The Silent Voice in Education

The Silent Voice in Education

The Importance of Involving Classroom Teachers

Vincent B. Troiano

ROWMAN & LITTLEFIELD
Lanham • Boulder • New York • London

Published by Rowman & Littlefield
A wholly owned subsidiary of The Rowman & Littlefield Publishing Group, Inc.
4501 Forbes Boulevard, Suite 200, Lanham, Maryland 20706
www.rowman.com

6 Tinworth Street, London SE11 5AL, United Kingdom

Copyright © 2019 by Vincent B. Troiano

All rights reserved. No part of this book may be reproduced in any form or by any electronic or mechanical means, including information storage and retrieval systems, without written permission from the publisher, except by a reviewer who may quote passages in a review.

British Library Cataloguing in Publication Information Available

Library of Congress Cataloging-in-Publication Data Available

ISBN 978-1-4758-4844-1 (cloth : alk. paper)
ISBN 978-1-4758-4845-8 (pbk. : alk. paper)
ISBN 978-1-4758-4846-5 (electronic)

I would like to dedicate this book to –

My mother Vera Troyano, my mother-in-law Connie Mulhern and my dear wife Connie Troiano – for their love of education and independent thought.

Contents

Preface		ix
Acknowledgments		xiii
Introduction		xv
1	The 1960s and "Change"	1
2	A Two-Tiered System	7
3	Local Leadership	17
4	Classroom Teachers React to the Times	25
5	Special Education: Basis and Reform	33
6	Classroom Management in Special Education	41
7	Education Establishment System Failure	49
8	Teacher-Initiated Change That Has Stood the Test of Time	61
9	Poor Leadership in Real Time	67
10	Special Education as a Bureaucracy	73
11	IEP as Legal Document vs Classroom Teacher Day-to-Day Evaluations	79
12	The Teacher as Facilitator vs Goals and Objectives	87

| **13** | Local Control of Education: A Beginning | 95 |
| **14** | Individual Instruction | 103 |

| Epilogue: The Classroom Teacher | 109 |
| About the Author | 113 |

Preface

Education in our country lost an opportunity to move forward in a positive manner when some parts of the education establishment moved too quickly with reforms in the 1960s. The promise of "new math," middle school, and special education as important developments for the future of education was taken seriously in our school district.

The fact that there was no sound basis of successful classroom instruction upon which the concepts were constructed was side-stepped. In that process, classroom pedagogy began to be ignored as necessary criteria upon which school programs should be constructed. Classroom teachers became the silent voices in education.

Personal experience with "new math" and special education are discussed in the book. Levels of bureaucracy that separate school districts from the kind of decision-making authority that would have made a difference in educational opportunity for many students is also discussed. More local control over state mandates would have been helpful, especially for special education students.

There can be no move toward local control of education without the "voice" of classroom teachers. Organizations and spokesmen who represent various agendas "seem" to represent "classroom teachers." However, only information generated by classroom teachers given directly to school boards would be the most reliable information of how they perceive their teaching environment. That information alone would, and could form the primary basis of movement to make local education more relevant to the student population.

Since the 1960s education has been moving in the direction of more control of school districts by outside influence. Common Core comes from the Federal level. Higher education has sponsored "new math," social studies, and special education. Teacher unions and labor negotiations have taken center stage and their spokesmen represent ideological, political, and legal attitudes not entirely supported by all they "seem" to represent.

An overreliance on education information from various parts of the education establishment outside the school district has minimized the influence of classroom teachers on curricula. As a result, there are many school programs, not the least of which is "new math," that even today exist in controversy.

The education establishment has moved in the direction of a reliance on "experts" beyond the classroom. The decision to have teachers attend seminars to recertify a teaching license is something that has little meaningful precedence from the past. In fact, the individuality of the teacher regarding classroom instruction was strong into the 1980s.

The impetus for writing this book was created when the education establishment deemed recertification necessary. In reality, that is just another effort to blame teachers for the failure of our education system to keep up with the evolving education systems in other countries.

The education establishment ignores Finland, where teachers have a leading role in deciding what happens in classrooms at the local level of education. It also ignores the action of some states, finding it necessary to designate as a matter of law, that teachers take part in curricula development.

There will have to be a new appreciation of teachers, and their role in a teaching environment, before there is a better future for education. This book "shines a light" on various failures of the system. The state, as one part of the educational establishment, is too many layers of administration away from a local school district to create mandates satisfying the individual needs of that district. Their "one-size-fits-all" approach fits few, if any, perfectly.

This book offers first-hand accounts, taken from a career in education, that highlight weaknesses in the system that account for much of the failure in leadership and programs. It's a classroom teacher's point of view of the forces that control the education system and are responsible for much of the "failure of education."

A move in the right direction can be as simple as a one-page report on curricula written by classroom teachers of each school in a district given directly to the local board of education.

It will help bring about conditions that once again focus on the concerns of the teacher in the classroom. Classroom teachers have a right to comment on curricula and other matters concerning their classroom.

Yet most, if not all, commenting and planning is done by "experts" with some kind of pedigree, maybe even an "agenda." Spokesmen for teacher organizations, school authorities with connections to, and sympathy for, various education approaches, even school curricula committees, can lead away from what most teachers in a school district believe is good education policy.

School boards will discover the way to create more local control, and thus more effectiveness of their school program, is to become closely involved in the issues most important to their teaching community. If local education is to move forward, a school board must take a deeper interest in school programs.

Their interaction with the administrative staff combined with information from the classroom teacher's point of view can form the basis of a very effective local school program. School administration on their own will represent general information from higher education and sources beyond a school district. Reports created by classroom teachers will bring back to education something that has been missing for a long time, unfiltered information upon which pedagogy used to be created.

A recommendation that school boards have the freedom to create a first-stage IEP (individual education plan) would be a good starting point for more local control. As described in the book it could create more special education assistance for a wider range of students.

In Finland, where special education assistance is not so tightly controlled as in our country, half the student population has received some special education assistance before they reach the upper-secondary level, which is close to the American high school. Guidance and psychological assistance are available in what we would call the elementary level. The demand for paperwork in our state leaves no room for such service.

Individual instruction, which is available in the resource room, offers personal engagement with the student, characteristic of the Finnish education approach which pays much attention to the individual student. Challenging school assignments crafted to the student's ability level which are open-ended can result in a very effective way of developing competency.

The education establishment in America must move to a better recognition of the value of classroom teacher evaluation of the education structure. A good beginning would be an appreciation of what has occurred in another country, when the resource called "classroom teachers" was given an opportunity to show what is possible in each classroom.

Acknowledgments

I would like to acknowledge the following people for reading my manuscript and offering poignant comments—
My brother-in-law Dr. John A. Mulhern, Kathy McDonnell, and Melanie Minch-Klasse.

I would also like to acknowledge—
My grandson Andrew Dobrow for the internet research and the Hunterdon County Library, Reference Department, especially Jane Ricketts for her help researching websites.

And a special thank you to my daughter Connie Marie and son-in-law Mark Dobrow for their patience, support, professional guidance, and occasional push.

Introduction

This book covers education from the early 1960s to the late 1990s. It is a story of how various parts of the education establishment blindly embraced the concept of "change" and the programs that resulted. Efficient delivery of instruction to students was affected.

Parts of the book are chronological and trace "change" created by teachers within the local school district, comparing it to "change" created outside the school district. Its main theme centers around the education establishment's gradual control of classroom instruction. Some chapters are dedicated to various aspects of curricula, others to failures of leadership.

Most of the information herein is drawn from a fairly, large school district with a good reputation. References to the education establishment are made with respect for the fact that it is not a monolith responsible for everything discussed. There is also a limitation in the fact that the point of view represented comes from one part of the education structure.

The term "perceptually impaired" describing students with learning disability was the original term used to describe some learning-disabled students. It has been officially changed to LLD, language and learning disability. The two terms are used interchangeably throughout the book.

Controversy exists to this day about the way in which classroom teacher efficiency can be increased. The fact that a multitude of different concepts continually surface indicates the depth and lack of agreement of the controversy. Classroom management skills and teacher-student relationship remain the leading indicators of successful teaching.

There is a need for classroom teachers to play more of a pivotal role in the creation of new programs so that local values are incorporated in such planning. The education system moved in the wrong direction for a long time because of the many actions explained in the book. For many different reasons teacher influence, "their voice in education," was silenced and has remained that way to the present time.

Chapter 1

The 1960s and "Change"

The 1960s began with three daily classroom elements that eventually disappeared. There was a reading from the bible that was gone before 1965. Recess in the morning and afternoon was out by the late 1960s. The Pledge of Allegiance gradually became less and less of a daily activity.

The disappearance of recess as a staple in the daily schedule is very interesting. Much of the recommended "change" of the 1960s came from the "top" of the education establishment structure. It's the reason for the "Top-Down" criticism that is so common. One excuse for so much acceptance in administrative circles is that the information from these "experts" represents the best of psychological and education thought. Yet, they seem to have "missed the boat" with a very important bit of information concerning the dynamics of learning.

Classes in elementary school in Finland are 45 minutes followed by a 15 minute recess for the first six levels of schooling.[1] According to a researcher, Eric Jensen, after high periods of attention, the brain needs a low level of activity (downturn) for new synapses to strengthen.[2]

That represents the newest information in understanding the brain. Recess in elementary school serves an educational purpose. It's a solid education technique which rarely, if ever, is discussed in this country as part of a purposeful structure to enhance learning. It was once a significant part of daily activity in the elementary school. That part of education planning was skipped over by the "experts" of the 1960s.

Education was expanding. Our school system went from a few hundred teachers to over 800 within a decade. Inside that expansion there was "wide acceptance" of what was considered "good for education," as it moved toward the future. Credibility was too easily given to ideas of preference rather than what had been successful in the classroom. It was too easy to be considered a "futurist" by denigrating phonics and traditional math.

According to the thinking of the time, "change" had to be addressed if a given school district was considered as entering the modern era of education. From the 1970s, and beyond, quite a bit of reorganization of education process was necessary, much of it was a correction to the overly enthusiastic reaction of the implementation of the "change" of the 1960s. In our school system, "new math" entered and was gone by the early 1970s.

Special education was introduced and grew exponentially. One early concept was "prescriptive education." It didn't survive the talking stage but was indicative of the theoretical nature of the considerations of special education at the time.

School law entered the picture. Those who understood the law were in a preeminent position. Negotiation of public sector contracts became a big business. They work closely with teacher organizations who have become powerful and are the leading spokesmen for the classroom teacher.

Higher education began to pursue various theoretical issues involving process in education. Programs that were touted as having a sound theoretical basis in education psychology began to show up in the classroom. Jerome Bruner, a theoretical psychologist wrote about curriculum reform and influenced theory emanating from higher education.[3]

The classroom teacher's relationship to the curricula changed, as the practicality of running a classroom started to take a "back seat" to ideas of a more theoretical nature. Higher education went "overboard," especially with Bruner's concepts about, "spiral curriculum," a way of gradually increasing complexity of information offered to learners.[4]

During the 1950s, research information began to emerge that identified the left hemisphere of the brain as the seat of verbal abilities and sequential information, and the right hemisphere of the brain as the seat of spatial abilities and holistic information. The whole truth is obviously more complicated, but this information is essentially true for most right-handed and a good majority of left-handed people.

Bruner wrote, *Essays for the Left Hand*, with this information in mind. Bruner had influence with those who looked to the "basic structure" of science and mathematics as the basis for building a more complete understanding of subject matter. At least, that was the belief.

The "experts" of the 1960s were highly qualified educators with a sincere interest in curriculum reform. They considered that their efforts could automatically improve education by adapting ideas from Bruner such as, "any subject can be taught to any child at any stage of development if it is presented the correct way." Thus, a deeper understanding was available to the student if the "basic structure" of a subject was uncovered and studied. Psychology theory began to influence education theory.

Morris Kline, in his book, *Why Johnny Can't Add*, responds that Bruner's idea was vague and led to a "docile acceptance of the abstractions on the 'new math.'"

Kline criticized the "new math" as, "concentrating on the superficial aspects of mathematics, namely, the deductive patterns of well-established structures, instead of emphasizing how to think mathematically, how to create, and how to formulate and solve problems." He concluded that, "school teachers should be the arbiters of what is to be taught and how to teach it."[5]

Higher education seems to have skipped over the fact that courses of study should be developed with the idea that they can be practically applied in the classroom. They forgot to realize theory was nothing but a first step in the creation of meaningful education reform. There is a distance between theory and the classroom called "reality." Proof, that the subject matter can be, and has been completely understood, must exist before widespread application takes place.

Teaching the various properties of mathematics did not produce the desired results in mathematics education. "New math," obviously an attempt to apply an understanding of the basic structure of mathematics was made available in the 1960s with the best of intentions. Our administrators bought the idea that the two approaches, the old and the new, couldn't exist at the same time so the traditional math books had to disappear.

At least, in our school district, the old books reappeared after five years, as the "new math" program was discontinued. "New math" programs continue in different places to varying degrees to the present time. There are reports that some teachers have resorted to teaching number facts surreptitiously in some places where "new math" still reigns.

Important questions about "new math" gained enough momentum over the years to have a president convene a Presidential Commission. There are not many definitive statements in the report of over a hundred pages. One that is of interest to those of us who worked on the elementary level and which this teacher experienced first-hand had to do with number facts.

The Presidential Report on Mathematics of 2008 indicates the lack of an ease of operations as existed in the past seemed to be hindering students from proceeding to higher levels of mathematics education.[6]

In fact, Kline presents the idea there is a difference between mathematicians in higher education who deal in pure mathematics and those who are connected to the education continuum. He claimed information from the latter group was presumptuous and did not belong on the elementary school level. Kline refers to the teaching of abstractions as wrong without concrete ideas in mind. He believed, "new math" was too conceptual.

Furthermore, there seems to be a conclusion, in the criticism of traditional math, that dealing with number facts is "rote" learning. Personal experience has indicated there was much more emphasis on understanding and problem solving at the elementary level than the critics of the traditional approach seemed to realize. In fact, brain researchers encourage memorization and some rote learning.[7]

It looks like school superintendents find a safer approach in staying "near" some kind of "new math" program, especially as part of a "vision" for the future. In an environment where classroom teachers have a "say," as in a school district interested in more local control of school programs, there would probably be a preference for more traditional activities in mathematics, or at least some proof of the efficacy of a new program.

In schools, and in countries where math is particularly successful, "time on task" is most likely involved. Yet, in Finland, their success is achieved with less time on task than in other countries. Their learning periods followed by recess must be considered as a significant reason. This teacher spent most of his initial time in teaching on the elementary level and experienced many positive aspects related to recess on the part of students.

However, most comparisons of learning programs indicate those who spend the most time studying learn the most. Thus, in places where more time is spent on math instruction, more math will be learned. In addition, countries around the world whose mathematics education is considered the best have fewer objectives to be covered at the elementary level.[8]

Social studies also began in the 1960s in the elementary grades, and "watered down" history and geography. It lacks the specificity that left children with a lasting impression of each subject that expanded as they progressed through the grades. Discussion with young adults also elicits the fact of no civic education in their background.

What happened to education in the 1960s and 1970s? "New math" was introduced and has failed because it is too abstract and the terminology is too confusing. In 2008 Congress was still trying to find out what went wrong. Special education was introduced and has gone through many adjustments to the detriment of the education of many students. Social studies replaced two subjects of substance, namely history and geography.

The concept of middle school education was introduced in the early 1960s. It was presented by theorists to address the needs of the preadolescent student. The idea included replacing junior high school, grades seven and eight, with school organization that included grades five to eight, or six to eight. Our school system considered grades six to eight for middle school. Local outcome will be addressed later.

The middle school education program of the early 1960s focused on growth between childhood and adolescence. Five main themes are: a home base teacher for every student; personal development of skills; individual progress with curricular options; interdisciplinary teams; and exploratory social development.[9]

In reporting progress of the reform, research of the early 1970s indicated without implementing multidisciplinary teams for instruction, the middle school would fall short of the goals of its advocates.[10] Questions still arise concerning what constitutes a middle school curriculum.

Cooperative education was also conceptualized in the 1960s. It has a long record of interest and much-touted success. Research reports are more careful and claim certain conditions must exist for it to produce these results. "However, if school districts expect that by introducing group-based mastery learning or Madeline Hunter's methods they can measurably increase their student' achievement there is little evidence to support them."[11] That is the statement of a researcher who supports the concept but wishes to stay within the boundary of actual test results.

A conclusion by Slavin, the professional who has studied the research states, many of the studies supporting the concept were not carried on for a reasonable amount of time. He is of the opinion, that for cooperative education to be successful there must be group goals and individual accountability and that must be a routine and central feature of instruction.[12]

He disputes the claim the effect of cooperative education is larger than one-on-one tutoring. There is no question about the positive effects of cooperative education but according to his interpretation of the research data, the actual effect is smaller than interpreted and only exists when the two conditions for teaching are met.[13]

The "change" of the 1960s moved education in the opposite direction of the classroom. Though many influential individuals in education agree with Klein that teachers should be the arbiters of what is taught and how it is taught, the education establishment view that they "know better" prevails. Teacher development programs, teacher accountability, and teacher recertification emanate from an establishment that refuses to consider teachers are not the problem. In Finland, they are the answer to the problem.

No one expects our education structure to emulate Finland's. We are two different societies. Their culture has more of a base in reading than ours. However, their success creating from within the teaching profession a viable education structure should not go unnoticed in America. Those who are responsible for various aspects of education should be ready to consider information directly from teachers as recommended in this book.

NOTES

1. Pasi Sahlberg, Teachers as Leaders in Finland, Educational Leadership, ASCD: Alexandria, Virginia. Oct. 2013, Vol. 71, No. 2.

2. Marcia Di Archangelo, The Brains Behind the Brain, Educational Leadership, ASCD: Alexandria, Virginia. Nov. 1998, Vol. 56, No. 3. An interview.

3. J. S. Bruner, *The Process of Education* (Harvard University Press: Cambridge, 1966). Copyright 1960 by the President and Fellows of Harvard University.

4. Bruner, *The Process of Education,* p. 52.

5. M. Kline, *Why Johnny Can't Add* (Vintage Books, A division of Random House: New York, 1974) pp. 121–122, 157, 204.

6. National Mathematics Advisory Panel, *Foundations for Success: The Final Report of the National Mathematics Advisory Panel* (U.S. Department of Education: Washington, DC, 2008) pp. xiv, 2.

7. Marcia Di Archangelo, The Brains Behind the Brain, Educational Leadership. An interview.

8. National Mathematics Advisory Panel (Singapore Math. Reference).

9. Thomas E. Gatewood, What Research Says About the Middle School, Educational Leadership, ASCD: Alexandsia, Virginia. Dec. 1973, Vol. 31, No. 3, pp. 221–223.

10. James Di Virgilio, Why the Middle School Curricculum Vacuum? ASCD, Alexandria, Virginia. Dec. 1973, Vol. 31, No. 3.

11. Robert E. Slavin, On Mastery Learning and Mastery Teaching, Educational Leadership, ASCD: Alexandria, Virginia. April 1989, Vol. 46, No. 7.

12. Robert E. Slavin, Research on Cooperative Learning: Consensus and Controversy, Education Leadership, ASCD: Alexandria, Virginia. Dec. 1989–Jan. 1990, Vol. 47, pp. 52–54.

13. Robert E. Slavin, Slavin Replies, Educational Leadership, ASCD: Alexandria, VA, April 1989, Vol. 46.

Chapter 2

A Two-Tiered System

Many different opinions, concerning the perceived lack of efficiency in the education system can be found in the literature. They range from the general proposition the entire system needs change to critiques of teacher skills. Amid this multitude of criticism, little attention is given to the management model that has evolved since the early 1960s. That model has not served the education community well.

The management model was supposed to be part of a system in which all parts interact equally well. In fact, something far different has developed. It has become a system in which communication goes one way, from the managers to the teachers. An appropriate characterization would be the "Top-Down" system because that is the way management works there. Classroom teachers do not have a "meaningful" voice on education issues.

Education leaders have been favoring theoretical concepts over the practical and time-tested aspects of education. The "Top-Down" managers paid too much attention to the supposed "experts" and their calls for "change" in education in the 1960s. The practical part of education, as represented by the accumulated knowledge of the experienced classroom teaching staff was ignored by the establishment, as an important consideration to any change that might take place.

There was a time when the best practices of the classroom were pursued. Those practices became the pedagogy that was education. It came from classrooms where experienced teachers were part of a system that respected continuity of well-established education programs.

Various methods and techniques were eventually accepted as standard. Teachers used them as practitioners of standard curricula.

However, that began to change in the 1960s. With the desire for rapid "change" in education, decisions were based upon psychology theory and education theory, rather than what was realistic concerning classroom instruction.

"Experts," mostly from higher education and theoretical psychology, preplaced classroom teachers as the spokesmen for curricula. Many of the "new" programs have either come and gone, or in the case of special education had to be continually corrected. In the interim, classroom teachers have had less and less of a say regarding "what" and "how" they teach.

The concept of classroom teachers as partners with school administration is unevenly applied because interaction is not a designated part of the system and classroom teachers have no official means to meaningfully influence their superiors in curricula matters. In some school districts interaction exists and the two groups work well together in an effective manner.

However, the extent of teacher influence depends on the "good will" of the administrator in charge. Small school districts naturally allow for more meaningful interaction among the teaching staff and administration. Information offered in this book came from teaching experiences in a large school district.

Since the 1960s, education leadership and more specifically what they call "change" has never measured up to what was expected. The public and some state governments has not only noticed, they understand something must be done. Maryland and California were the first to introduce legislation that designates classroom teachers an official part in the process that chooses curricula.

This book is an attempt to add a classroom teacher's perspective to the consideration of reform in education. It's a personal explanation of how various decisions within the system, from the state, down to the local level affected the capability of classroom teachers to deliver their programs to the best of their ability.

Teachers, especially those with experience, must be considered an integral part of all phases of the education process. Their skills are wasted when they are used to merely carry out programs created by the changing philosophies of the chosen "experts of the time."

One of the controversies that emerged in the 1960s had to do with comprehensive high schools. They were touted by most parts of the education establishment as an aspect of American education that was being accepted around the world. The full spectrum of society could be addressed in one high school and all social levels could interact.

Some parts of the education establishment wanted to have high schools that concentrated on education closer to work requirements. There were various groups that addressed the issue as early as the 1950s. One of them, the National Panel on High School and Adolescent Education in 1976 recommended moving vocational training out of the high school and into the workplace.[1] Various commissions made other recommendations, one of which was vouchers.

Those who backed the comprehensive high school won the debate and those schools remain the main source of high school education to the present day. The objective of moving high school education closer to the workplace or even developing a closer relationship with industry seems to fit the immediate needs of society presently being discussed. A board of education might want to assess the needs of its community before it decided which was best for the students in their local school district.

That is exactly what is done in Massachusetts. The state does not have high school graduation requirements. If a community has as much as ninety percent of its students move on to college after graduation, which was the case in Massachusetts, teachers were involved with the community in creating appropriate graduation requirements. A situation that fit the community was created because of the freedom given by the state.[2]

The middle school concept, which was championed in the early 1960s has had an interesting history. The expected development in a standardized specialized curriculum never materialized. As of 1973, it had not developed an interdisciplinary approach among teachers and the only difference in most school districts between junior high and middle school has been the make-up of grade organization, five to eight, or six to eight, essentially housing two different schools.

New concepts of the education of adolescents were discussed and used as a motivation to build new schools. Team teaching, cooperative lesson planning, and more attention to the individual student as a developing adolescent were offered as some of the advantages to the new school setup. The use of a multidisciplinary approach has proven to be more of a challenge and depends upon dedicated individuals who are strongly committed to it.

Even team teaching, and team planning have been found to be a highly individual concept and is more likely to be successful among those who create it. The proper interpersonal relationships necessary for the success of such programs are usually taken for granted. They may be part of an original planning stage but are not easy to sustain. Even the yearly change of some personnel creates new challenges.

Reports concerning long-term success indicate there are insurmountable problems that inevitably develop. Apparently, much of what was conceived as middle school education is now block teaching with teachers responsible for their own classes. Instead of criticizing the various directions which school districts have taken, maybe there should be a realization that the original conceptualization of middle school was flawed when imposed from above. Most likely, where it now is successful as a middle school program close to the original concept is in school systems where classroom teachers have made it work from within.

It was another of the ideas that originated in the 1960s outside the classroom teaching community. The growth between childhood and adolescence was the focal point and the middle school program was to address it.

There were trends to expand certifications for middle school teaching from 1973 to the 2000s. Florida required a middle school certification to be achieved before 1975 to teach in one.[3] Yet, at that time there was still confusion as to what constituted a middle school curriculum. The concept of teaching to the individual seems to be entwined with multidisciplinary teaching along with student choice.

As of the year 2000 there were reports of difficulty and confusion in what constituted a middle school curriculum. There are widespread differences among teachers and administrators about the present state of middle school education. And research indicates that without a multidisciplinary approach it is not a true middle school program.

Classroom teacher evaluation in a curriculum report would present the most up-to-date information. A board of education that has the confidence of its teaching staff that all information on curriculum is dealt with in a responsible manner could gain a fresh look at the concept. The original plan seems to have been an outgrowth of the "change" of the 1960s and exists differently in various school systems. A definitive definition as to what really exists locally would be beneficial in developing more appropriate education planning for the future.

There was a good deal of excitement in Florida concerning middle school education in the mid-1970s. The concept grew rapidly. Yet, in the early 2000s an alternative approach was chosen by a Florida school district to address a certification problem.

They started with one K-8 school in 2004–2005 and as of 2016, according to reports, has at least nine K-8 schools. In 2005, a discussion with one of the teachers involved indicated they were able to produce good opportunity at the seventh and eighth grade level. In addition, there was advantage in transportation because many students from the same family could be picked up at once. Good behavior was a natural result of the more natural atmosphere in Port St. Lucie.

It was the freedom of choice that allowed the county school board to pursue an alternative solution. They solved an education problem with satisfactory results. It's a good example of what can happen with some local control.

In a well-meaning effort, our state created a special education system that put thousands of children in self-contained special education classrooms. With the growth of special education, teaching programs came about in colleges to develop special education teachers. The creators of these programs thought they knew about special teaching techniques and materials that were above and beyond what classroom teachers knew. They were wrong.

This teacher relied on much information, especially individual instruction, gained in the regular classroom to create opportunity for the special education students with whom he came into contact. Nine years teaching on the elementary level created a sound basis to work with the learning disabled. There was a natural expectation of achievement from teaching in the regular classroom that did not seem to exist among teacher trained in special education.

Much of the material upon which special education considered as a base for instruction was too simplistic to be developmental. It has been reported that now more modern special education teaching materials are more appropriate. How could they be much different from regular class materials matched to the student's reading level used in the past? Hopefully, the new materials are not geared to group instruction.

In addition, there seems to have been no requirement to develop good understanding of students in the regular classroom. It has been reported that some special education teachers began their career with certification for the regular classroom. It would probably have been beneficial to develop regular classroom experience before taking over a special education class. Expectations of behavior and achievement seem to be different in those entering the profession from special education teacher training.

From the early 1970s until a major correction was made years later, special education students fell behind in skills when they were in self-contained special education classes. The higher education part of special teacher education did not deliver what it had promised.

The "experts" also gave us "Open Classrooms." Schools were built to suit the concept. That was a learning situation where two, three, or four classes might be in a large area without walls to separate them. We experienced a large room with a movable wall between two classrooms. There was an expectation that we open the wall and do things with both classes at once.

We knew that less than five percent of classrooms in England, the home of the concept, utilized the approach. The local administrators said classroom teachers were "resistant to change"; that program also disappeared after a few years but not until a school was built to fit the concept.

Before the mid-1960s, in elementary schools, history and geography were taught as independent subjects. Both disciplines result in valuable concepts. That changed in the 1960s with the creation of social studies. History and geography in the elementary school started to take a backseat to other concepts. We were never given an explanation about why such a change took place. As of an earlier reference, it looks like an adaption of one of Jerome Bruner's concepts of teaching advanced concepts in a "spiraling way."[4] It was a theoretical attempt to advance the student's thinking without information about the efficacy of perceived outcomes.

In a video of a talk at a college in Texas, Jacques Barzun an educator of note commented on social studies as an elementary school subject. One of his conclusions was that the effort to introduce a smattering of disciplines was not successful because among other things some of the basic concepts are too complex to present at that level.[5]

Apparently, to Professor Barzun there is quite a "glitch" in the concept of "spiraling," maybe some concepts thought of as simple don't lead to increasingly deeper understanding. Ask a student about World War I, or the Civil War. In the past when history was an elementary school subject, elementary school students could furnish information about those events. Today, college students are perplexed about the time-lines of those wars.

Elementary school mathematics had also been deemed needy by the "experts." They have consistently redefined mathematics education since the mid-1960s. Many times, the excuse given for failure was that classroom teachers need more training. The fact is the "experts" were not objective. They took for granted the idea that learning basic structure of mathematics would automatically lead to a deeper understanding. In fact, new math has more terminology to learn than traditional math.[6]

A common element of each of these attempts at "change" is they were instituted from the "top." They were not classroom teacher driven. One excuse usually given for the lack of success of some programs, and an overall lack of achievement in general, is that classroom teachers lack the necessary teaching skills.

The same system that created "change" to improve education without the desired results provides in-service education to classroom teachers to "develop" more skill in teaching. Personal experience has indicated the best teaching skills were found among experienced classroom teachers.

One excuse for in-service training for teachers is that, "there certainly are some poor teachers in the population." The concept of using in-service training to make the required adjustment has a flaw. It's using an across the board technique while it has already been proven that the most efficient training focuses on specific goals tailored to the individual.

Large numbers of poor teachers, if that is indeed the case, and if they have been properly identified, are a problem for administration. It's their duty to identify poor teachers and do something about it. Is one to believe the education establishment will correct poor teaching by showing everyone how it is to be done? Do they really expect to make the needed corrections among the "poor teachers" they describe as the reason for the program?

There is a specious aspect to the argument, "we need better teachers." If the situation is as bad as some in the education establishment claim, it was accomplished on their watch. "We need better teachers" is really the education establishment declaring to the public, they have done a lousy job monitoring the situation. How can they be expected to fix it?

Another indication of the chasm between education administration and the classroom teacher is the way teachers of the year are treated. "I thought they might be interested in a discussion of education and all they wanted was a photo op. It was over in a minute." That's a reaction of some recipients of teacher awards.

It's a reflection of what the upper echelons of education and politicians presently think about the worth of the classroom teacher's view of education process. It would be refreshing to have a teachers' conference outside the purview of some political agenda. Whereas speaking at a union conference would be "preaching to the choir," a presentation at a state board of education meeting would garner some important attention.

It might bring back more of an interest in what is happening in the classroom. Classroom teachers, since the 1960s, have had less influence in education than they had in the past when more attention was paid to the pedagogy of the classroom as a base for teacher education.

The rallying cry of administration that "change is good" has proven to be an attitude on their part that is too cavalier. When classroom teachers are left out of the process of "change" or if their effectiveness is compromised in the name of "change" the public is being "short-changed" by special interests that have become increasingly powerful in the periphery around education.

A classic example of interference in basic education process is the ongoing attempt to pursue programs that offer alternatives to phonics instruction in the teaching of reading. Teachers are sometimes told to move away from phonics because," the students are tired of it," and, "there are better ways of teaching reading." Teachers don't hear students say they are tired of phonics, just a few administrators.

Experience with phonics over the years was positive. In fact, the longer one teaches the more one appreciates the advantages that a good phonics program offers students. In addition, students have always responded energetically to various phonics drills, even in group instruction in special education classes, where getting a group to work together is not always an easy and efficient means of delivering service. The criticisms of phonics have never been credible. Yet, some programs, and some "experts" continue to try to minimize its use.

When classroom teachers are forced to minimize the use of basic teaching tools like phonics because of the personal preference of an administrator, they are not at fault if there are poor education results. They do not need in-service training. They are being victimized by poor leadership. If phonics returns to education on a broader basis, it's because of classroom teacher demands. A recent report indicates that is happening. Yet, it has taken decades for the excesses of the 1960s to begin to be corrected.

One of the miscalculations that led to so many missteps on the part of leadership was an overestimation of the value of anything that came from higher education. There was little if any attempt to balance theoretical concepts against the practicality of implementation. If it came from higher education, it was thought to be valuable.

This overreliance extended to "expert" advice when it came to hiring school superintendents. "They should have a vision to bring the school system into the future." That's reasonable. How it is approached is another story. School superintendents have an average career of about three years in our state because the "future" has a different definition to too many people.

When it depends on too much of the promises of the past, it is bound to be disappointing. A closer connection to the "grass roots" of a community would be looking within the community for the kind of information that will help lead to a better future.

Education is not the only part of society that has lost touch with the "rank and file" of its constituency. When there are too many layers of administration of anything, inefficiency develops. If each teacher's individualized skill is minimized by declaring there is only one correct way to teach effectively, the American education system will continue its "downward spiral."

Classroom teachers and school principals once worked together with a mutually agreed upon curricula. That commonality started to break down in the 1960s. The role of the classroom teacher started to change. The "Top Tier" of education began to tell the other "Tier" what to teach. Many years later, in reaction to the poor result, the "Top Tier" decided to take complete control.

Now, the education establishment wants to teach teachers "how" to teach. It's an abdication of the responsibility of administration to use the excuse there are enough poor teachers to create a system where all teachers must be recertified. It's their responsibility to identify problem teachers and do something about it.

A school principal with a responsibility for the program of a "school" instead of being a member of a superintendent's "team" would be more likely to interact with teachers in accordance with a "locally" influenced curriculum. Looking to complete a superintendent's "vision" for the future by instituting a "modern" curriculum without classroom teacher participation, is another reason why education has not been moving forward.

NOTES

1. Daniel Tanner, *The Comprehensive High School in American Education* (Education Leadership, May 1982) pp. 606–613.

2. The National Mathematics Advisory Panel, Hearing, Committee on Education and Labor, House of Representatives, one hundred tenth congress, second session, May 21, 2008, Serial No. 110-93, p. 52.

3. Paul S. George, *Middle School in Florida-Where Are We Now?* (Education Leadership, Dec. 1973) pp. 217–218.

4. J. S. Bruner, *The Process of Education* (Harvard University Press: Cambridge, 1966).

5. Jacques Barzun, Video from a talk at a college in Texas.

6. M. Klein, *Why Johnny Can't Add* (Vintage Books, A Division of Random House: New York, 1974) pp. 121–122, 157, 204.

Chapter 3

Local Leadership

One outcome of "change" was a new concept of the school principal. Prior to the 1960s a lifetime educator of considerable classroom experience was usually chosen to be a school principal. That principal was the education leader of the school, with a deep knowledge of, and a strong allegiance to its education program. Both the teachers and the principal had a lot in common. Their backgrounds in education allowed for a unity of purpose.

There were regimens that were standard, recess: fifteen minutes in the morning and fifteen minutes in the afternoon. It was one of the first things to become expendable in the 1960s. In fact, one of the commissioners of education in our state considered doing away with physical education in the schools. Yet, if one were to look at available information concerning the advantages of exercise for the body and the mind, it would be difficult to find a rationale to limit it with young children.

Curiously, the only change in the era of "change" that involved physical education was to mandate coed classes. Immediately, physical education teachers began reporting the boys didn't want to play rough around the girls and the girls didn't want to run around in front of the boys.

If there were local control of education, the local school district could decide what was best for their student population. Thus, the ideas of limiting or encouraging physical exercise would have a chance to be explored by strong proponents on each side of the argument. Why should the state have the last "say" in the controversy if there is not a right or wrong decision? It's a matter of values that a local school district should be able to decide on its own.

State education commissions have minimized the influence of individual decision-making by creating too many "one-size-fits-all" mandates, usually with too many objectives. That's one reason why education has not forged ahead in this modern era. Too many things to consider does not allow for the concentrated effort in some areas to make a measurable difference.

The state is too far away from local decision-making to sponsor policies that are appropriate for individual school districts. Many objectives in course and program guidelines has been the states' way of trying to cover "all the bases" on a wide range of topics. That's another reason for a lack of achievement in testing and other situations. School districts should have the freedom to create their own emphasis in various areas of their control. Especially in elementary arithmetic, fewer objectives has proven to lead to more success in measurable achievement.[1]

The classroom teachers of a school district offer a vast resource of information concerning education. It is there waiting to be tapped. Instead, the education establishment almost compels the states to get too involved with teaching and instruction at the local level in unnecessary ways. The most egregious intervention is the business of teaching classroom teachers how to teach through their mandated in-service.

Teaching the quick effortless recall of arithmetic facts didn't seem to be a problem before the 1960s. The President's report on mathematics recommends the "quick effortless recall" of math facts in response to much of "new math" which includes the memorization of terminology connected to the designated properties of math.[2] Yet, even the president's report is contradictory in that it asks for fluency with facts throughout the report, yet it encourages the understanding of the properties, even in the same paragraph.[3]

Understanding the properties of mathematics has been tied to the complaint that there is too much terminology. Words could be the enemy of instinct which allows for immediate recall when dealing with number facts. Obviously, the president's report is a compromise that allows various parties to mathematics education have their ideas put forward but without a consensus on the best way forward for mathematics instruction.

Boards of education are left with a choice. Is the best information concerning education in local classrooms? How much should they rely on the education establishment? As local school boards become more involved with their school programs and interact with their classroom teachers this will become evident. Boards of education will view leadership in a different light as they realize their teachers reflect the best information available about the students in their community.

Rather than sending out new principals to "make teachers work," they will have a better concept of how to foster leadership that enhances their education staff. Chosen leadership should reflect the community, not try to change the community.

What do you think happens when a superintendent of schools is chosen according to a "vision?" In our state they last on the average of three years.

Politics is usually given as one reason why there is so much dissatisfaction with school superintendents. Another reason is they only have a short window into which they have the chance to show or prove their program will work.

During the 1960s, the new concept of the school principal became one in which he/she is part of a "team" headed by the district's superintendent. The team works together to further the superintendent's plans for the school district. That new focus was centered on the superintendent's "vision for the future," usually accompanied by a call for "change."

The modern principal was to be long on personality and public relations skills. A lifetime commitment to the classroom was no longer necessary. How does one choose to be a leader at the early stage of a career? Lack of experience affects decision-making.

Reliance on forces outside the school district affects what happens in classrooms inside a school district. Too much confidence in education programs "in vogue" is connected to the idea that "change" is good, a characteristic of many modern school principals. "Change" is only good when it brings about improvement. Truthful scrutiny of the supposed improvements of "change" has never occurred at a significant level.

Commitment as a team player puts too much emphasis on uniformity. That defeats professional independence as a sense of purpose in creating the best education that can be offered in a school. You could become an elementary school principal with as little as one or two years teaching experience in an elementary grade.

The qualifications for such a position state otherwise. Yet, new principals arrive in schools as the leader with preconceived notions that indicate little attention was paid to finding education beliefs that match up with the experienced teachers of the school. The practice that allows these administrators into a school has led to less vigorous scrutiny of the programs entering the school. Such a case will be discussed later in the book.

Independent principals with more classroom experience and more individual school responsibility could have been an effective "firewall" against the debilitating effect of poorly thought out programs of "change." Many students were negatively impacted as a result. Lack of discussion concerning responsibility for the failures of the past indicates a cavalier attitude toward education that does not exist among classroom teachers who work with students daily.

The new concept of the school principal impacted education on a grand scale and worked to limit classroom teacher influence in the schools. Without a strong connection to an in-house curricula it was easy to implement education programs that were touted as being successful in a nearby community.

Boards of education that communicate with their classroom teachers will have first-hand knowledge of what goes on in their schools. They will be on the "same page" with their principals and teachers. Boards will have to realize no one is going to give them the education they want for their students. They must learn to coordinate the education that comes from within the community to that which is available from outside the community.

Bringing in a new superintendent of schools every three years is not managing an education system. It's reinventing the wheel. School administrators, in general, represent a comprehensive point of view of education created mostly from education establishment sources far removed from local classrooms.

School superintendents in our state with an average tenure of about three years have little time to get their "vision" going. Their promise of "change" that offers a better future for the school district usually coincides with the same information provided by the "expert" advice which comes from education establishment sources.

School board members might better acclimate a new superintendent to a tenure longer than three years by being able to relate and discuss information which inherently possesses values and needs of the school district. Boards of education seem to rely on a new vision to come into their school district and create a transformation. That's not realistic. Yet, besides politics, it's probably the main reason why disillusionment sets in with a new superintendent.

Failure by the local school board and administration to be in close contact with classroom teachers led to such things as individualized reading introduced to us thirty years after we introduced it in our classrooms. Local control of education implies a process that is built from the ground-up. Complete freedom from state control is not realistic. However, more authority to make a mark on local programs is a necessity if there is to be "change" driven by local values and the needs of the community.

Different areas of the country have a variety of needs concerning local opportunity for employment. Internship programs could become a part of local education if school boards presented to their state reasonable plans developed with participating industries. Vocational programs in schools built for that purpose were called for before the 1960s but the comprehensive high school became the education of choice because of backing from influential leaders in education at that time.

There seems to be a need in the current business climate that was the inherent concern of one school of thought of the 1950s. Specific skills for the workplace may be more important now than when the curricula for a comprehensive high school was adequate for a different generation of students.

Local control of education will only bring about the desired change where boards of education assess the immediate needs of their school population and strive to build relevant education programs. That has not been accomplished under the guidance and influence of the education establishment. The school principal as the education leader of a school should be pursued in the future. It would serve as a strong basis for appropriate local control.

As a member of a "team," the principal only serves interests beyond each individual school. School principals at a meeting discussing the needs, interests, and values of their individual school would be the definition of local control. School principals at a meeting discussing the superintendent's "vision" and how to incorporate it into the school program could be one reason why the average residence of a school superintendent in our state is of a short duration.

A board of education with more specific information from their teachers will better represent their constituency. The political nature of the position should be affected by a much broader understanding and a deeper involvement in the specific information that is the core of local education.

Another area of concern is curricula. Our state, during the era of "change" gathered information concerning what math skills were taught in the fourth-grade statewide to create a grade-level test. There was quite a zealous response that was too expansive regarding the teaching of skills.

A test was created that covered everything reported. Few, if any, students could pass it because of the broad areas it covered. That attempt was quite outside the norm of test development. Too many objectives in math and other subjects are increasingly being identified as a reason for the dilution of effectiveness in teaching and learning. That is another area that can be changed. Limiting objectives in state guidelines can free boards to put their own mark on courses of study.

As special education was developing in our state, there was a need for the local school district to deliver to the state, curricula for the self-contained special education classes that were on the planning board. A great deal of paperwork was created. It had to come from psychology books most of which had to do with abnormal psychology studies. At that time, there was little to no past practice to describe, because what eventually became the special education bureaucracy was in its infancy.

The original classroom theory of special education was flawed and years later mass mainstreaming of students involved in the program resulted. As reported elsewhere in this book, special education materials, in general, were too simplistic to be developmental. Personal experience in a self-contained class for students identified as emotionally disturbed found regular school materials geared to the student's reading level were more than adequate. Individual instruction was a necessity. There was too much of a range of abilities in each student.

One advantage of individual instruction in the special education classroom and the resource room was the ability to use a variety of learning materials. Not only do students have varied learning problems, they also react to various learning materials differently. Members of a board of education that have such first-hand knowledge of what is going on in the classrooms of their school district can choose a school superintendent that "fits" their concept of local instruction.

If the special education laws had been more precise about responsibility and boards of education were delegated specific authority concerning special education students, negative conditions that had to be revisited over the years would never have been allowed to develop. A lot more in now known about special education students and the best practices to insure their development. It's time to revisit the issue. There would probably be a lot less political pressure if there was strong local consensus regarding the school curricula centered around local needs and local values.

An agreement in that regard would shift the focus from looking for answers in education outside the school district to creating curricula and programs from within the school district that defines the individuality of the school district.

Thus, a board of education would be looking for sound leadership instead of a new direction every few years. Being able to define the needs of the individual school system to the commissioner's office to achieve more local control would be a good start in looking for a new school superintendent.

The extraordinary administrative skills of those who qualify for the position of superintendent of schools might better be used to create a conduit with the state department of education. Interpreting the attempt of a school district to define its individuality within the structure of the state department's concerns could break new "ground" in creating solutions to problems in education.

Finally, there are the members of the school board who at times are accused of using that position to vault to higher political positions in the community and beyond. Refocusing the board as more of a center of education activity will make it more closely involved with classroom teaching and less political. A deeper understanding of the school program can only broaden the scope of understanding of the learning process in those involved.

If education in America is to keep up with the rest of the world as it improves its ability to educate its young, America will be forced to find a new paradigm for education. Tapping the acumen of its classroom teachers will lead in a much better direction than the turn downward that started in the 1960s.

Donald J. Noone in his book *Teachers vs. School Board* states, "schools have been set up to educate the young 'in loco parentis'." (in place of the parent) "this idea in most state constitutions has encouraged local control of the schools." "These decision makers are generally called the school board and their chief task is to set education policy, prepare the school budget, and insure the proper running of the schools."[4]

His book is about teacher militancy and is sponsored by the Institute of Management and Labor Relations, an extension of Rutgers University. It offers information concerning teacher organization relations with a board of education with the consideration that others will learn from what happened in that situation. "Although this research is not designed to develop an action program that would facilitate this end, the possibility of learning by analogy exists."[5]

That is the exact concern of this book. Hopefully, enough information about education on the local level will be presented to raise the concern of interested parties, especially school board members and parents, about the lack of effectiveness in the past.

Too many layers of administration from the state are compounded by the number of school districts for which the state remains responsible. Local school administrations and state administrators are too closely tied to higher education and the various learning programs they present. School boards are too closely tied to teacher organizations and their spokesmen. School law and litigation should not so easily intimidate local school boards into thinking they must listen to the "experts" in each of these situations.

A one-page report from their teachers or something similar that serves the same purpose is the information a school board needs to know exactly what is going on in their school district, no spokesman, no ideology, no ulterior motive, pure information.

A school board can be more of a center of education policy than an institution that seeks to follow mandates made in distant places in general terms for a broad spectrum of society.

NOTES

1. President Commission Report, p. 21.
2. President's Commission Report, p. xiv.
3. President's Commission Report, p. 27.
4. Donald J. Noone, *Teachers vs School Board, Research Section, Institute of Management and Labor Relations, University Extension Division* (Rutgers University, MacCrellish and Quigley Co., Feb., 1970) p. 1.
5. Noone, *Teachers vs School Board, Research Section, Institute of Management and Labor Relations, University Extension Division,* p. 8.

Chapter 4

Classroom Teachers React to the Times

It is foolish to attempt radical "change" without including in the planning process everyone who would be affected. Yet, that is exactly what happened one year in our school system in the mid-1960s. When we arrived for classes in September our math books were gone and in their place was a modern math program. The program had to be abandoned after four or five years. It was a case of administrative prerogative taking the place of solid educational thought, too much enthusiasm with "change."

When we were being introduced to the replacement textbooks a few years later the salesman said they were similar to our old math books. The new books were put together by their editors from books of the type used in the past. The reason given for the replacement of the "new math" program by a traditional program similar to our old one was, they found the "new math" program was too abstract for the bottom third of an average class.

That was the standard excuse from the education establishment. There were conceptual problems which necessitated a presidential commission that gave a report in 2008. As reported elsewhere in this book, there is one paragraph in the report that essentially supports the traditional and the "new math" approach.

Maybe a comment on some personal experience at the elementary level can shed some light on problems presented to those who tried to teach it. In sixth grade, where the division of decimals was introduced, renaming values was extremely time-consuming. The program presented reasoning in the place of automatic procedure. As a result, the process was not efficient at all. It was very cumbersome and took a long time. There were rows and rows of numbers. It was confusing and had to be done on a blackboard slowly and accurately.

If a real need existed to change the mathematics so completely, then it would probably have been a better idea to start it in kindergarten and let the program follow the students up the grades. However, the replacement program would have to be decisively more efficient than what it replaced. Since it is classroom teachers who must answer for the scores on standardized tests, they should have a voice in the selection of such programs. It's foolish to think such a move could be accomplished without their input.

Surely, Kline's book questioning the supposed deductive reasoning and his explanation of the politics involved would have made decision-makers look for more proof of efficacy before committing a school system to the "new math." Our school authorities made the decision to scrap the approach five years after it was introduced. In hindsight, it was an honest response to questions of competency of the method.[1]

The Kline book was published three years after our school authorities' perceived difficulties. If the math program were a state mandate, a correction would have taken a lot longer. The school district's decision was a good example of the need for local boards of education to have the leeway to make corrections to state mandates that might adversely affect their student population.

Classroom teachers most likely would not condone as much "change" as administrations would like. But whatever they did consider would have a much better chance of being successful and surviving the test of time. That's a safeguard for school systems not an impediment to "change." Kline believes, appropriate consultants can be involved but should not lead the work. "schoolteachers should be the arbiters of what is to be taught and how it is to be taught."[2]

Another area where administrators can have their way is in the committee process. That's why some states want to designate classroom teachers as an official part of curriculum planning. Presently, education committees can be used as a "smoke screen" to further the administration's point of view and make it look like consensus. It's common in education to have a textbook appear in a school system that was not the first choice of the committee. There is nothing to stop an administrator from overriding a committee decision.

Apparently, a more modern approach involves curriculum committees, and textbook selection committees, comprised of master teachers, principals, and parents. There was a committee that chose the modern math program that only lasted five years in our township.

That is why something like the one-page report on curricula mentioned at various times in this book is important. Too many times a spokesman for an organization offers opinions that may represent the ideology or theoretical considerations of a governing board that is not in line with the thinking of most its constituents. A good example is the lack of consensus among teachers about the use of their union dues for political donations.

The Supreme Court has finally made the determination and teachers are no longer subject to the few who have their own agenda regarding union dues.

Thus, the power of the organization, used to further thought of the few has been set back in that instance.

Information obtained directly from classroom teachers represents the most accurate information available concerning school curricula. Properly used, it can form the basis of a better future for a school district. No matter what the education establishment tries to "pass off" as the only way to effectively teach, experienced classroom teachers, with appropriate freedom, develop the most accurate means of delivering instruction to a student population.

A board of education dedicated to developing as much local control as needed to advance curricula shaped for the benefit of their student population, would benefit much more from locally created guidelines as opposed to mandates from a state bureaucracy.

Effective "change" is probably best achieved within the purview of existing school programs and with the advice and consent of existing staff members. In fact, in some places, "change" goes on all the time in reasonable situations and no one needs credit.

Teachers are seldom recognized as those who have brought about "change." However, many an administrative career has been "made" when a person is considered an "agent of change." That title sometimes is enough to give status to the individual even if the efficiency of things that were changed was not thoroughly scrutinized.

There was once a time when "change" was not such a "flash" word. Improvement was simply a byproduct of changing times and done naturally. It did not exist as a driving force for its own sake. During this teacher's first year in education it became apparent that the students in that initial fourth-grade class were extremely proficient at phonics and there was no longer any reason to present a phonics lesson during the reading time.

The students, in general, could read accurately and well. The school principal was approached and asked if an independent reading element could be incorporated into the reading program as an alternative unit for a period of time.

That doesn't seem startling in the present world. But the time was the early 1960s and the principal had been a teacher for forty years. In fact, he refused to be a full-time principal, insisting on teaching half a day. He liked the independent reading idea and on his own asked the PTA to purchase more books for the library to support it.

This "old-time" principal, according to the "thinking of the time," was supposed to represent the group of educators who were impediments to "change." That's why forward-looking administrations of the day couldn't wait to retire him and others like him and replace them with people who were ready to be part of a "team."

The "old-time" principal represented an education system in which the school was a cohesive unit. The administrator and teachers worked within a framework of mutually agreed upon curricula. Prospective teachers of his time taught a "time honored" curricula, a pedagogy that had become standardized. And though at times boring, it was effective in teaching the basic skills necessary to educate children. When teachers were hired in his day, they brought with them methods and techniques that were fairly standard in most schools of education.

One might expect that a school principal from that time would not be flexible when it came to a change in the standard curricula. He accepted the change because it made sense and was a sign of the times. Children's literature was becoming more accessible and individualizing instruction was on its way.

The change was smooth and effective because it was done within the structure of the ongoing reading program. Individual reading took the place of the regular program for a while. Some of the initial comments of the students were, "I didn't know this was reading," and "I read a hundred pages last night." It was apparent that individualized instruction could unleash a good deal of student initiative. One girl related, years later, that she eventually read all the biographies in the library.

There was also information pertinent to learning disabilities that would be worth investigating. Some poor readers did not visualize the events they read about in a story as well as most other students. This was obvious when they tried to make illustrations for a book they had read. In fact, in one case a student who had a most severe reading problem had no concept of figure-ground. When he tried to copy a still life of a bowl of fruit his pictures were the only ones that had the fruit scattered around the picture instead of piled in the bowl. That's why learning disability is individual and complicated. Is it related to perception or something else?

One of the most valuable outcomes of this experience was learning the importance of feedback. So much work can be produced by students that the program can get out of hand if care is not taken to see that there is a systematic way of dealing with what has been read.

This scenario had to have been playing out in many other schools, because within a year book companies were providing classroom libraries to be used for independent reading. It was a simple idea: begin to provide for individual reading experiences after a sound basis in phonics has been achieved. Most classroom teachers appreciate it. The times were calling for it. Yet, as happens in so many cases, there were those who went "overboard."

That's when various programs started to emerge that minimized phonics. There was an in-service program, years later, during the 1990s sponsored by our school board in which a young college teacher was showing us how to use individualized reading down to the first-grade level. After the meeting, we talked. She was born in 1964 and was told it was done with fourth graders in our school system in 1963. She was gracious and said, "I believe you." We discussed the need to teach skills at the early elementary level.

She wasn't really trying to sell us the idea of an individualized reading program at the first-grade level, just to introduce it and present some appropriate materials. A professional concern would question the value of time spent on individual reading at the first-grade level. There would be a need to balance out the time spent on skills development, which would have a better long-term payout. Fourth-grade students with a sound basis of phonics had no problem taking full advantage of an independent reading program.

A more pressing question would concern the disconnect between the school board's introduction of individualized reading, in 1990, to its own teachers that did it in 1963. If the school board and the school administration had a better idea of what had been going on in their school district the reading program on the elementary level would have been in a much more sophisticated state. The lack of knowledge about such things is a characteristic of "Top-Down" management, the information only goes one way.

A seventh-grade teacher in a middle school once related an interesting story. One year the students in his class were excited by the independent reading approach. He had them using library books and the various reading labs in his class. For some reason they attacked the work with more than the usual energy. Their reading scores were quite high on the standardized test given at the end of the year. His statement was, "The scores were the highest in the county."

The statement wasn't pursued to find if the scores were actually the highest in the county or if he simply meant they were probably the highest in the county. His main point was that not one person in the administration came to him and recognized the fact of the extremely high scores. None of them congratulated him or even wanted to know what he did. A school system based on local control would pursue anything of that nature which would increase their efficiency.

That teacher's success could be interpreted or explained in two important ways. First, "time on task" is one conclusion used to explain success when learning programs are compared. Students who spend the most time studying learn the most regardless of the method or methods involved.

Second, the program was open-ended. Students continued with the tasks on their own. Both are valuable learning tools not always open to a classroom teacher.

The fact that classroom teachers were reacting to advances in education thought is in stark contrast to, "we need better teachers." There were plenty of teachers capable of doing the same thing. Many of those who were allowed, did it. The system, however, does not allow for such freedom to surface on an equal basis.

At another time, in true "top-down" fashion, a modern school principal, with only a few years in the classroom commented on a request to institute some individual reading in the fourth grade of his school in an inquisitive manner. Claiming his "territorial imperative" from behind his desk, he asked, "How will they learn the correct skills?" Apparently, he was closely connected to the various lessons that were part of a series of directed lessons in the reading program in use in that school.

It is not known if he had something to do with picking that program. He seemed to have a sense of security with it and a sense of insecurity with delving beyond the scope of the program. Curiously, he didn't appreciate a need to have fourth-grade students branch out to a broader area of reading. The principal who taught for forty years didn't have that same sense of insecurity to expand the parameters of the reading program.

During this same time period, reading programs were coming to the market that either downplayed or even eliminated the use of phonics. Teacher complaints forced the addition of supplements that included lessons in phonics to suddenly appear. Apparently, over the years, according to recent reports, that township has moved even closer to phonics in the teaching of reading.

How do such reading programs appear in a school system that were so quickly and blatantly rejected by teachers? Without inside information one must conjecture that a salesman sold the program either to an influential administrator or to the board of education.

Some administrators, at times, gain enough influence to encourage the purchase of programs that are outside the purview of what most classroom teachers prefer.

How can things like that happen in a school system? The emerging constant in education is that classroom teachers are being told to function within a system that is determined by others concerning what is good for the classroom.

There was another case which might demonstrate the classroom teacher in the forefront of "change." It involved personal experience, emerging information on behavior, and an adjustment to a phonics-based spelling program.

A fourth-grade student offered a predicament for the child study team (CST).

There was behavior disorder in which the student didn't seem to care about anything and had some problem getting along with the other students. In addition, there was learning disability. The CST favored a diagnosis of emotional disturbance.

There seemed to be attention deficit disorder (ADD) but his social problems did not have the personal intensity this teacher observed while teaching classes for the emotionally disturbed. His problems with other students were more in the vein of random events. For example, a student who is emotionally disturbed would be more likely to take offense to a certain student or certain situations and have emotionally reaction to them on a regular basis.

The student didn't have such particular emotional reaction. He might kick the student in front or behind him in line as a reaction to something that may have just happened not as a pressing and continuing psychological reaction to a particular situation.

The quandary for the CST was unique. At the time there was no official designation for ADD. The state had not yet added it to the list of classifiable learning disabilities. In addition, the CST did not believe ADD existed without hyperactivity. Personal observation indicated the student fit the pattern of other students who were easily distracted. We usually put spelling programs and language programs on a tape recorder for such students.

Discussions with other special education teachers indicated they were aware of the same predicament. The CST had no official way of identifying students as ADD. Those of us who had taught in the regular classroom were more familiar with such students.

In this case no hyperactivity was observed along with the easy distractibility. The CST believed ADD did not exist without hyperactivity, probably because they were relying on the state code or lack thereof. Eventually, ADD became an official designation. And it can be designated as with or without hyperactivity.

This is another situation in which time for real "change" had arrived and once again classroom teachers were in the forefront. The use of tape recorded programs for students with ADD was started by special education teachers and is also another change that has weathered the test of time. There is another dynamic of special education involved here. In reality, students should receive instruction based on their education needs not on their identified disability. This teacher would have provided programs on tape for the student no matter what his disability was called by the CST.

The student reacted well to the spelling program that was put on tape. The constant auditory stimulation was enough to keep his attention from wandering. It enabled him to stay on task long enough to get some continuity in his efforts.

In this case an interesting event happened. His reaction, the first time he got a hundred percent correct on a spelling test, was observed by accident. He very quietly said to himself, "Yes" while pushing his arm down under the desk in a kind of victory celebration. It was not done for anyone to hear. The teacher just happened to see it.

This was a student that hardly showed emotion about anything. He really did care. The lack of emotion was partially a cover for not being able to successfully do his grade level work. Those of us who were teaching in special education classes and had been regular classroom teachers had a reservoir of experiences with which to compare student achievement and behavior with that of the special education students we met.

We had a good idea how children identified with learning problems were similar to students in the regular classroom, and how they were different. We knew which behaviors needed to be addressed and those that were no different from other students. Yet, we were never tapped for contributions to the planning and organization of education programs. That was one reason why it took years for state and local education authorities to react to certain problems in special education.

True local control of education can be built on a close relationship between the board of education and its classroom teachers. The reaction of classroom teachers previously discussed indicates teachers respond to the times in a more efficient manner than the education establishment. A board of education owes its student population immediate attention as opposed to waiting for the state to attend to an issue.

A lot of time is spent planning from both a practical and theoretical basis by competent and caring educators. However, it seems that the farther away from the classroom operational plans are made, the more likely is the possibility of problems developing. In asking for the correction of problems from afar, as in the state level, too much time is lost with those affected.

The longer it takes for needed information to reach the correct source, the more harm that takes place. The state made corrections to special education almost twenty years after problems surfaced.

Close contact between classroom teachers and the board of education can minimize the time it takes for programs that are not living up to expectation or "hype," to be identified. Thus, interruption in achievement that occurred in the past will be minimized. Corrections are more likely to take place in an environment where a local school district has an "individual" relationship with the state. Locally created programs within a broad state outline would be easier to correct than programs created by the state that must be corrected across too many levels of administration.

NOTES

1. Morris Kline, *Why Johnny Can't Add* (Vintage Books, A division of Random House: New York, 1974).
2. Kline, *Why Johnny Can't Add,* p. 204.

Chapter 5

Special Education
Basis and Reform

No one told teachers to implement changes that have stood the test of time, discussed in this book. Better ways come from inside the classroom. The time for these changes had come and classroom teachers, with the freedom and opportunity, brought them forward. Modern math, one of the moves, in the era of "change" that was imposed on many classrooms in the 1960s, is still in "limbo."

The early 1970s saw the beginning of special education classes without the policies that eventually gave so much control over programs to CSTs. In some ways and for some students the early years of mainstreaming in special education were the golden years. It was not highly organized, and the special education student was an integral part of a classroom program. Teachers welcomed such students because they took part in the placement decision and had confidence the student could benefit from their program.

If the attitude of classroom teachers has changed it is because the procedure has changed to the extent that now the teacher has no recourse if the CST places a student in their class to the detriment of their program. Rules regarding the placement of special education students have become more rigid over the years, giving the CST even more authority over a school program.

Other conditions in special education also changed. The resource room teacher was not allowed to see the CSTs social worker file about the student without a special request. The person who spends the most time with the student and knows the most about that student's intellectual development is not "privy" to information gathered by the school system. One time in conversation, a remark about a student looking like his father was returned by the mother that the child was adopted.

If a school system is to gain some degree of independence to have curricula that represents in some way their uniqueness there will have to be movement on the part of the state to give that township more control over the CST bureaucracy. It is no secret the CSTs produce tons of paperwork that is never utilized. A simple change in procedure could make the special education student closer to the regular school program and bring more local control to the board of education.

The principal, classroom teacher and resource room teacher of a school could easily handle a first-stage IEP that is not covered by the law. Students could be supported quite satisfactorily in a normal resource room program without close supervision by a CST. Coordination within the staff of the school and flexibility of programs would allow the special education student to be a part of the regular school program with a minimum of special education identification.

The CST could be in closer contact if problems arise and a second stage IEP would be created to address serious issues. Then, an IEP protected by state law might be more appropriate. That would bring about a more judicious use of CSTs. It would cut down on all the yearly or even two-year reviews that take up so much paperwork and time for everyone involved. The original intent of CSTs was to bring the unique qualifications of the professionals involved closer to students. It was envisioned as more of a "hands-on" service than something that was in business to simply keep writing reports.

Such an approach would have the possibility of expanding service to students in a few ways. It would free CSTs to spend more time directly involved with students or would allow for fewer CSTs and more resource room teachers. It might even free psychologists to provide counseling service on the elementary level. The most efficient aspect of education, time spent with students, would allow for a better education environment.

The experience of being an elementary school teacher then becoming a special education teacher might help explain the personal belief there is too much emphasis on the special education aspect of identifying students and closely tying them to an IEP. Time spent with problem students led this teacher into special education with the idea of functioning as part of the school program. In fact, that is the way we functioned in the early years of special education.

As the special education bureaucracy grew there was more emphasis on the student as being part of special education instead of being part of the regular school program. Eventually, there was more and more CST control over the students in the resource room program.

This teacher began a career in special education in a self-contained class for students classified as emotionally disturbed, in 1970. Previously, nine years were spent teaching grades four through six. The first special education class had five students. After a week of working with them and observing their behavior it was apparent that individual instruction was the best and probably the only way to effectively teach them. Skills gained from previous experience with individualized instruction were a great advantage.

There were five boys ranging in age from about seven to nine. Two had diagnoses of a severe nature. A boy with the diagnosis of Autism was one of the two. The other boy's diagnosis indicated a thought disorder. He did not display a severe learning problem. Three other boys had been in the first grade of different schools. They were in that class because of emotional and behavior problems. They, along with the boy diagnosed as Autistic displayed learning problems.

The youngest student in the class was the Autistic boy. He was bussed in from a nearby school district. The only way to keep him directed to a task was to have him sit next to the teacher at a table for the complete time he was in school. Instruction was carried on at the table when the teacher was not circulating the class attending to each student's individualized program. The students either came to the table or the teacher went to their desk.

The Autistic boy spent only one year in that class as his school district instituted a class into which he was incorporated the next year. His parents and this teacher developed a friendship through which the student was referred to a medical clinic that treated his problem with mega-vitamin therapy. Eventually, he developed to the point where he could hold a job in a franchise food business.

His inclination to put his two hands together when attempting to write gave one the idea that the two hemispheres of the brain might have something to do with that reaction. By having him put his left hand out of site, at times in his pocket, his right hand did not seem so hindered when it came to the attempt to write something. That led to investigating the literature that might shed some light on the matter.

The result was a study on handedness. It showed a lack of differentiation in handedness of students in classes for the emotionally disturbed when compared to students in the regular school setting. The study was good enough to produce a master's degree and an offer to publish it with the professor. It was never published.[1]

There was intent to extend the study with perceptually impaired students to see if the same dynamic was involved. That was the reason for enrolling in a doctoral program at a nearby university. However, the state began to change the rules regarding access to students and their personal files. The researcher no longer had access to information concerning IQ, age, and such, all necessary in comparing groups involved in such research.

Research for the study led to Samuel Orton. In some circles he is considered as the inspiration of special education because of his work with students who had problems learning to read. He was a physician very interested in learning disability. He did so much research that now he is considered as a neurophysician. In some texts he is referred to as a neurologist. He helped develop the Orton-Gillingham method of teaching the learning disabled. Part of it is described in this book as the method used with students of the very low functioning group in a class for the emotionally disturbed.

He created information concerning the hemispheres of the brain that has relevance for education, especially special education. Without knowing the exact medical information available today, he figured out the relationship between the verbal hemisphere and the nonverbal hemisphere of the brain.

Presently, it is understood that the normal relationship of the two hemispheres of the brain is one of asymmetry. The usual cerebral setup in the right-handed person is one in which the left hemisphere controls verbalization and the right hemisphere is the seat of spatial, or nonverbal abilities. The temporal lobe of the left hemisphere of the brain, with more surface and volume, controls verbalization, that hemisphere is usually referred to as the leading hemisphere.

Galaburda, a medical researcher who has studied dyslexic brains, states, in discussing the temporal lobe of each hemisphere of the brain, it is "asymmetric in two-thirds of the population, fails to show asymmetry in dyslexics in most published studies."[2] Rather than talking about size or weight the researcher simply indicates the temporal lobes are asymmetric in two-thirds of the normal population yet symmetric (lacking in difference) in the dyslexic brain.

That is what Orton means when he refers to the "lack of strong lateralization, essentially a lack of differentiation, of the two hemispheres of the brain" He believed it, "resulted in various conditions from gifted abilities to learning disability and behavior disorder."[3] He figured out characteristics of the two hemispheres of the brain and was eventually proven to be correct according to scientific research.

The author's study on handedness supports Orton's theory. Students in classes for emotional disorder showed a lack of differentiation in handedness that was significantly different from students from regular classes. If one accepts handedness indicates a relationship with the appropriate hemisphere of the brain, then the lack of differentiation in handedness in a motor-cognitive area could show the same kind of relationship between the two hemispheres of the brain.

Orton believed the lack of differentiation (symmetry identified by Galaburda) leaves the individual susceptible to stress which may have something to do with students being in a class for the emotionally disturbed.

Other researchers who believe a lack of differentiation in the hemispheres of the brain can result in emotional reaction are Palmer and Zangwill. Palmer found subjects who had a highly developed preferred-hand skill also had better psychological adjustment. Those subjects who tended to be ambilateral (an absence of recognizable developed dexterity in either hand) generally described themselves in a maladjusted way. The term "awkward" was used very often by the group displaying ambilaterality, while it was not utilized at all by any member of the other group. More aggressive feelings were also measured in the ambilateral group.[4]

Zangwill claimed ambilaterality doesn't imply abnormality in psychological development but the possessor of that type of organization is particularly vulnerable to the effects of stress.[5]

Orton believed the nondominant hemisphere could interfere with the acquisition of language if there was not enough of a lateralization (separation) of abilities. In other words, if the temporal lobe of the nondominant hemisphere interfered too much in language acquisition, learning disability resulted. A confounding aspect, which Orton realized, is the nondominant hemisphere can learn words but is not able to functionally use language.[6]

Sperry, in the 1950–1960s, a researcher who studied the brain, was able to prove that if the important nerve fibers that connected the two hemispheres of the brain were cut, two different brains resulted. His research substantiated the language abilities of the left hemisphere and the spatial abilities of the right hemisphere in most people, along with the ability of the nonverbal hemisphere to learn words without the ability to use them in verbal language skills.[7]

Various possibilities for the reasons for learning disabilities brings into question stringent plans for improvement by diagnosis. Orton looked at the popular reading method of the early twentieth century, the sight word approach. He did not question the fact that it seemed to produce results with beginning readers. He was concerned that simply learning words worked in reverse for that segment of the student population that did not have a strong degree of lateralization of the two hemispheres of the brain.

He compared two communities which used the sight word approach to teach reading. The community that used phonics to help students who had trouble learning to read with the sight word approach had half the amount of what he described as retarded readers as a similar one that kept students involved with sight words until they had learned them.

He concluded the sight word approach with certain students might even make their problem worse. If the nondominant hemisphere were involved in learning words, it had no way of using them in verbal language. He believed that could in fact hinder the dominant left hemisphere's ability to develop language.[8]

The preceding information offers some background information regarding an effective education approach for the learning disabled. The population that fits the patterns previously discussed may be similar in that they possess symmetry regarding the hemispheres of the brain, but the manifestations of that condition are diverse. In fact, Orton, in the early part of the twentieth century, was also ahead of the times in declaring "Dyslexia is not a disease entity; it is a name for a range of variability for language acquisition."[9]

The first-stage IEP takes into consideration the variability of learning problems and the value of addressing them early in education. The exact classification is unnecessary and is secondary to addressing the need that surfaces. A comparison of approaches in dealing with the learning disabled will lend support to the first-stage IEP discussed in these pages.

Finland has a very active special education program that begins as the student enters school. Guidance and psychological services are available immediately. Students receive service according to need. The service is increased as needed. The student might eventually be assigned to a self-contained special education class if the need arises. That is an option that does not occur very often. Apparently, all special education personnel are involved with students, who remain close to the regular school program.

In America, special education is presented in a very different manner. There are personnel who only test and diagnose students, referred mostly from elementary classrooms. An IEP is produced which is supposed to be a guide to an instructional plan for the student. At times, there is a waiting period for the CST to get to a student because the structure of the program is paper-intense and time-consuming. The system is inefficient and does not provide the wide range of service that could be provided if more professionals were directly involved in teaching students.

Whereas, need is the reason students in Finland are given assistance, classification is the requisite for special education assistance in our system. Discussion in this book about ADD indicated special education teachers were responding to need with ADD students before there was an appropriate CST classification. Special education teachers are responding to need when they use the IEP as a guide, really a starting point. It certainly is not a curriculum, nor should it be.

The resource room in America offers a most appropriate approach to deal with the learning disabled because the individual instruction responds to the need projected by the student. A place where CST diagnosis must be careful is recommendations and a proscribed learning program that is too restrictive. The most effective part of resource room instruction is the ability of the teacher to find and use the materials and approach through which the student can find success. There is such variability in each learning-disabled student that limiting the teacher's ability in any way to deal with the student is a disservice to that student.

The IEP as an initial set of recommendations may be helpful. The inability of the IEP to serve as a curriculum is discussed in other sections of the book. Special education made another mistake when resource room teachers were no longer allowed to talk to classroom teachers regarding the mainstreaming of special education students. That was simply the action of a bureaucracy creating more "turf" to control. In Finland, special education teachers coordinate with classroom teachers.

The wide range of materials available to the resource room teacher can easily support classroom programs but with an individual approach that is for the benefit of the student within the structure of the classroom teacher's program. The lugubrious weight, upon education programs, of the special education bureaucracy, has really limited service to elementary school students. Every student does not need a battery of tests to qualify for some assistance. The earlier it is given in a student's career, the sooner the student begins to receive the full benefit of schooling.

In Finland school principals consider themselves as one of the staff and many teach. Trade in most of the special education bureaucracy for resource rooms in each school in our country, and education will have made a giant stride forward. Students in elementary school at times must wait years to receive classification. Whereas, with expanded resources, students will receive attention as early as assistance is needed. Education progress for the special education student is really through service not testing and classification.

NOTES

1. Vincent B. Troiano, "A Comparison of Handedness in Normal Children and Emotionally Disturbed Children," Master's Thesis, Newark State Teacher's College, May 1973.

2. Albert M. Galaburda, *Dyslexia 5:183-191* (John Wiley and Sons, Ltd., 1999) p. 186.

3. Dr. Samuel T. Orton, "The Sight Reading Method of Teaching Reading as a Source of Reading Disability," *Journal of Educational Psychology* February 1929: 135–143.

4. R. D. Palmer, "Hand Differentiation and Psychological Functioning," *Journal of Personality* xxxi (1963): 445–461. Psychological studies involved were Minnesota Multiphasic Personality Inventory (MMPI) and the Taylor Scale of Manifest Anxiety.

5. O. L. Zangwill, *Cerebral Dominance and its Relation to Psychological Function* (London: Oliver and Boyd, 1960) p. 25.

6. Orton, "The Sight Reading Method of Teaching Reading, as a Source of Reading Disability," 135–143.

7. R. W. Sperry, "Hemispheric Specialization of Mental Faculties in the Brain of Man," in Claremont Reading Conference Yearbook, xxxvi, 126–136.

8. Orton, "The Sight Reading Method of Teaching Reading, as a Source of Reading Disability," 135–143.

9. Margaret Byrd Rawson, *The Many Faces of Dyslexia* Annals of Dyslexia (The Orton Dyslexia Society: Baltimore, Maryland, 1986) Vol. xxxvi, p. 180.

Chapter 6

Classroom Management in Special Education

The expertise of the classroom teacher is the skill of managing students, whether it be a roomful or individual instruction, the regular classroom or the special education classroom.

Teachers make programs work, within reason. That's why the excuse of "not implemented properly" is unreasonable. It's an excuse that is an outgrowth of modern forces that believe they know a better way.

Special education was in its infancy in 1970 when this teacher began working with a class of students identified as emotionally disturbed. The psychologist, of the CST involved with the students in the class previously discussed offered some advice. He said, "Give them M&Ms when they do something good." That was all he had to offer. Apparently, his experiences had something to do with Skinner, a behavioral psychologist, who was involved in behavior modification through appropriate rewards.

There was not much more psychology had to offer special education at that time. A word of caution, when this teacher tried some reward therapy, the students quickly wanted to know how much of a reward before they attempted a task.

Experience from regular class instruction, especially in individualizing instruction was a better preparation than one could have ever imagined. There was not that much known about dealing with special education students in a learning situation at that time.

It was 1970. The Autistic student had a file that claimed the child's problem resulted from trauma over the father's death. More accurate literature on the problem developed over the years. His mother suspected he was born in that condition. Curiously, at that time, there was quite a bit known about the behavior of such children, such as demanding everything in life stay on a strict schedule. He would know if items in his room were moved upon his absence. Science eventually supported the mother's suspicions.

Special education in 1970 was not as closely controlled by the bureaucracy as in later years. All interaction between the special education teachers was on an informal basis. There was never any regular routine where we were brought together to share what we had learned with each other and the administration. The lack of communication between teachers and administration and its effect can be demonstrated by a discussion with a school principal in the mid-1990s, some twenty years later.

His school had a few classes for young students identified as emotionally disturbed. There had been many problems there over the years. A discussion elicited the fact about the problems. In response this teacher's experiences were related about how individualized instruction helped control behavior. Another dynamic was to limit interaction between the special education students and try to have them experience interpersonal behavior in the regular classroom as much as possible.

The principal said they were starting to do that. The response that it's twenty-five years later was not taken lightly. He turned and walked away. We never spoke again. Though the principal took it as an insult, the fault does not lie with him. It lies with the special education bureaucracy that was never up to the task of understanding classroom management.

In dealing with a group of students identified as emotionally disturbed one cannot expect them to have good interpersonal relations with the other students in the class. They are there because they couldn't get along in a regular classroom situation. It's not reasonable to assume things would be different in the special education class.

Their opportunities for normal interaction came when they were mainstreamed in regular classes. Even those who were not ready to take part in an academic class could get some benefit from art, music, or physical education. Individualized instruction allowed for education development and diminished the amount of interaction between students. Conflicts were kept at a minimum.

After a few years in special education it was time for a practice teacher. The class of emotionally disturbed students at the time was especially tough. In fact, it was impossible to leave the practice teacher alone in the classroom even after she was ready to oversee the class on her own. It was necessary to sit in the back of the room and monitor the situation. That led to much note taking and offered the opportunity to sit together for about 15 minutes every day after class and discuss the day's events.

The experience showed just how many skills an experienced classroom teacher possessed. One does not really appreciate how much has been learned about education until it is contrasted to the actions of a very talented but inexperienced prospective teacher. The complexity of controlling behavior and delivering instruction develops naturally in the classroom teacher. It is an underappreciated skill.

Special education administrators in general and others that would create classroom programs that are not familiar with classroom management make assumptions that are not realistic. The fact that an experienced classroom teacher possesses a high degree of skill in classroom management as well as the ability to successfully teach lessons is often overlooked.

Seminars that profess to teach teachers how to teach deny the individual achievement resulting from each teacher's maturity in the profession. The education establishment's attempt to have teachers teach according to their specifications contradicts the conclusions of early researchers who understood there was a variation to good teaching that defied a one-size-fits-all mentality.

That belief was still strong in the 1980s when there was discussion by state officials trying to decide how to best evaluate classroom instruction. "Teaching is a complex activity. . . . the instructional supervisory process must accommodate different teaching styles and learning situations within the context of each classroom."[1] That was quite a different concept of the classroom teacher in 1986 than what the education establishment would have the public believe about teachers today.

Regarding individualized instruction, the practice teacher related that they did not teach such skills to her in college. That was the early 1970s. She was a bright girl and had no reason to mislead on the issue. If that is accurate then it is further proof that classroom teachers were really in the fore front of providing meaningful "change."

Before the 1970s, most of the information available in psychology had to do with abnormal behavior as opposed to dealing with students with learning disability. Orton's work was centered around "reading disability." Special education was conceptualized as covering a broader range of dysfunctional behavior. That was one reason why there was a time when higher special education was telling teachers to use such things as art therapy and other hands-on approaches with special education students.

Special education was given a broader mandate than the amount of credible available information should have allowed. They miscalculated the abilities of special education students and underestimated the extent to which these students could handle academic work.

Our state created a vast network of special education. Years later when the national ideal proposed mainstreaming as necessary, we were accused of being behind the "times." In trying to stay ahead of "the curve" we wound up "behind the eight ball."

The next stage of special education involvement was to graduate special education teachers who were supposedly more understanding of learning disability than the classroom teacher. The expectations of the special education bureaucracy that self-contained special education classes would attend to education problems outside the realm of, or even the ability of, the classroom teacher was completely mistaken.

A psychologist, on one of the CSTs at the time, even expressed the belief that the self-contained classroom experience would accelerate the student enough to have that student move into a normal classroom situation ready to achieve on grade level. That was the early special education promise.

Prior to contact with this practice teacher another important aspect of special education and especially individualized instruction had been addressed. Special education materials were too simplistic to be developmental. Fourth-grade level reading books that were written on a second-grade level, so as not to stigmatize an older student, also did not educate him. Basal materials (i.e., regular grade instruction books and programs written for a specific grade level) were more appropriate.

Instruction materials written for a regular third-grade program were superior to materials written for a fifth grader reading on a third-grade level. There was no challenge to reading and understanding how to proceed on an individual basis with the simplistic materials, on the part of the student. A student who can read above the second-grade level can proceed with learning materials that require some independent decision-making on the part of the student.

The only thing necessary to make them part of the program was to seek out those materials or make them. A wide range of teaching materials and appropriate programs that kept the student interested and challenged were easy to assemble. Integration into regular classroom programs was the goal. The materials and methods used were geared to that future consideration.

In the mid-1990s, the situation changed for those of us who worked as special education classroom teachers at the middle school. The state changed the rules and regulations concerning such classes. They were responding to the call to mainstream all special education students. It had become common knowledge the longer students were in special education classes the further behind they fell academically. There was a great deal of pressure to do something.

As a result, most special education students and their teachers wound up in regular classroom programs for a good part of the school day. The change was a move in the right direction. However, it was not well planned. We were told to report to various classrooms where some special education students were now assigned. The regular classroom teachers were also a little confused because they were not completely clear on what was expected from the special education teachers in their class.

One of this teacher's assignments was a reading class in which a regular class reading teacher wound up sharing his program. The charge was for the special education teacher to help special education students in the class with their school assignments. That did not give the special education teacher enough to do, so we each taught part of the program. That worked out very well.

Another assignment was in a language arts class. That teacher was extraordinarily good at his trade and it was foolish to be taking up any class time that he might spend addressing the class. Therefore, very little was done in that class. It was a shameful waste of this experienced teacher's time.

The "most telling" part of this experience was the reaction of a special education teacher who never was a part of a regular classroom learning situation. He was assigned to a math class which contained students he had taught the previous year in a special education class. One day in discussion he said, "I had no idea these students were capable of doing what they were doing."

Essentially, he was reevaluating the special education college experience that taught him that special education students were different. He found they were not much different from students in regular classes. That was something that special education teachers who had been regular classroom teachers had known all along.

The mainstreaming previously discussed occurred as an attempt by the state to correct a by-product of the special education consideration that self-contained classes would result in better skill development in the students they classified.

In general, special education administrators did not have much of an interest in mainstreaming during the early 1970s. That was a time of a noticeable increase in the number of self-contained special education classes. An especially high number of students were diagnosed as emotionally disturbed because the state gave more state aid for such students.

The confusion created by the last-minute mandate of mainstreaming on the part of the state made it look like the local school district didn't know what they were doing with their special education students. The state's lack of monitoring the special education bureaucracy was the real problem.

The fact that IEPs are protected by state law creates a quasi-supervisory role for the CST. Instead of being on equal terms with education elements within the school system, the CST has the last word in education situations. The conditions in self-contained classrooms continued over the years because "that was the realm of special education." Boards of education were as perplexed about how to proceed just as were school principals.

This teacher's first special education class, in 1970, was previously discussed. It was for students identified as emotionally disturbed and included five boys with varying diagnosis that at the time considered them to be emotionally disturbed. Within a month, one of them was mainstreamed into a second-grade class for reading.

It was the early 1970s, and even though the idea of mainstreaming special education students in regular classroom programs was new at the time the classroom teacher involved was very supportive. Her attitude was one very common to classroom teachers. She felt a responsibility to the student once she decided he could take advantage of instruction in her class.

Another boy of third-grade age, who was reading at a first-grade level, made progress that year. The following year arrangements were made to have him bussed to his homeschool each afternoon to spend a half day with a fourth-grade class. The principal and the classroom teacher were very cooperative and patient. The student had somewhat of a dour temperament with some temper. However, he survived in the school setting with cooperation from school authorities. In sixth grade he won the science prize at a school competition.

A third boy also of third-grade age who was reading on the first-grade level in that first class went back to his homeschool on a full-time basis after two years in that class. The number of students in the class always ranged between five and eight.

All the mainstreaming was initiated by the special education classroom teacher. The consideration, on the part of the special education teacher, was to be adjunct to the regular classroom. For students in self-contained classes, the idea was to find situations in the school program where they could function, then place them there.

Regular classroom teachers and school principals were always supportive mainstreaming the special education students into their programs. In fact, they felt it was their duty to provide regular class instruction when the student was able to take advantage of such. That was in the early years, the 1970s.

As time went on CSTs became more involved in mainstreaming. The special education teacher was no longer allowed to talk to classroom teachers concerning the placement of students.

All mainstreaming had to be done through the CST. The emphasis changed from the special education teacher and the classroom teacher agreeing on a placement to one in which the CST decided where students would be placed. Eventually, CSTs gained even more control. Once a class was chosen, the classroom teachers had no choice.

The early mainstreaming looked to have the special education student in a regular classroom program in which that student is an integral part. The "new mainstreaming" included classroom teachers providing remedial services to special education students placed in their classes with or without the assistance of aides.

Rather than finding some way in which a balance could be found between the right of the regular classroom teacher to carry on a disruptive free program and the right of a special education student to be mainstreamed, the state rules favored inclusion over all else.

The state solution to the disruption of regular classroom programs was, and most likely still is, in-service training for the classroom teacher. Their experts would show the classroom teacher how to handle problems such as disruptive students and the time element (i.e., the extra time needed to deal with the special education student). That is simply the state's way of shifting blame to the classroom teacher for the untenable situations it created in some classrooms.

Most of the time, the experienced classroom teacher is cognizant of what is needed. They know when their ability to deliver effective group instruction is being shortchanged. What they most often need is a better allocation of services, not in-service.

Discussions with classroom teachers have given some not so surprising results. Contact with the learning disabilities specialist of the CST does not often offer many illuminating recommendations. What is possible within the limitations of dealing with a classroom full of students has usually been considered by the teacher before it becomes part of the usual "intervention strategy" offered by the LDTC of the CST. Presently, if teachers give the CST a list of what has already been tried, classification of the student might be accelerated.

More resource room teachers and fewer LDTs would most likely serve the student population in a more effective manner. If that were the case, more students would receive assistance in a prompt manner.

In fact, Finland has a robust special education program of assistance right up to their upper-secondary level. Almost half the students who get to that level have received some special assistance. They do not seem to have the stringent classification requirements of our special education system. Assistance seems to be available as soon as the need becomes evident.[2]

A first-stage IEP offers more flexibility to the school system. Instead of a teacher left to "make the best of a problem situation" one less CST could mean three to four more resource rooms.

It's really service to students that counts in education. More resource rooms offer the possibility of the individual instruction that provides for appropriate education development and allows for a more normal school atmosphere.

Contact with self-contained special education classes at the middle school level in the early 1990s made it obvious they shouldn't exist. There were problems caused by the existence of the classes and very little regarding positive results.

Students in special education had a conscious awareness of being segregated, much more than at the elementary school level. The behavior was kind of a swagger that told others they had some control over their lives. The instructional end was difficult to achieve with continuity because the lowest common denominator had to be addressed. A wide variety of problems were made impossible to address because improper behavior is contagious.

A tough student with a severe diagnosis once agreed to sit for five minutes with hands folded before being allowed to go to lunch. He asked to sit in the back of the room out of sight of the door. He said he couldn't afford to have anyone see him like that. His behavior was part of the student's need to project a certain image among his peers. He knew he could have the disciplinarian overrule the decision but agreed when it was pointed out he would lose time with his friends in the lunchroom. The teacher simply wanted him to experience sitting quietly for a few minutes.

By mid-1990s, as previously related, the state moved the focus of special education instruction at the middle school from self-contained special education classes to the regular classroom. The role of the special education teacher in those situations then became one of support. It was a move in the right direction. But it was too many years in coming.

Truthfully, the change came about more because the self-contained classes at that level were in crisis. It was made to improve the instruction of middle school students after the fact of crisis. It highlighted one problem with the state leadership. There are too many layers of administration between the classroom teacher and the commissioner's office.

Personal classroom experience indicated the best thing that could be done for the special education student was to see to it that he/she was kept as close to the regular classroom as possible. The state on the other hand had allowed special education to get out of hand through the mistaken idea that learning disabled were best served in the special education classroom.

It took years for the reality to emerge. The CST approach is one of individuality. A realistic approach to managing a classroom situation has never been their expertise.

In a locally controlled program, changes mandated by the state would not be necessary to bring relief to the kinds of problems previously described. Those programs got out of hand because the state was a higher authority than the local school district. There was no clear line of authority that would allow the local school authorities take over jurisdiction.

If local control of education is to be achieved the state will have to allow special education and regular school authorities to communicate on equal terms. The first-stage IEP not covered by state law will allow resource rooms to function as an extension of the classroom. Individual instruction is the best way to improve the education outlook of the LLD student. Special education resource room teachers can bridge the gap between the regular classroom and special education and create a more natural education situation for learning-disabled students.

NOTES

1. *NJEA (New Jersey Education Association) Review*, November 1986.
2. Pasi Sahlberg, *Finnish Lessons* (Teachers College Columbia University: Teachers College Press, New York, N.Y., 2011).

Chapter 7

Education Establishment System Failure

In the early years, the 1970s, special education grew so much that in some places it was almost a system within a system. In our school district many low functioning special education classes were created on the elementary level. "Testing" told the CST team certain students could not function in the normal school setting. Whatever they decided was backed by the law. Here is some first-hand information about two students from one of these classes and how they escaped.

In each case, the parents decided to insist on inclusion in the normal school program against the advice of the CST. Their children had been in first grade in special education. They were now second-grade students, and both were nonreaders.

After the students were placed in second grade in our school, the CST claimed the students could not be included in any of the second-grade reading classes. The resource room teacher was to provide all instruction. That was not the usual protocol. Students were usually given a chance to see if they could take advantage of some classroom instruction with other students.

With the principal's backing, a second-grade teacher included them in her reading class. The students were put in her low functioning group. She found they were able to successfully partake in the class. We then did something that was frowned upon at the time.

We double-dipped them (i.e., provide another dose of reading instruction during the school day). The state rules did not allow for that at the time. The students were well behaved and thrived. They progressed and were able to take advantage of some of the regular school program. Their disability, though severe, did not preclude them from being part of the regular school environment.

In fact, one of them eventually became the best resource room student (a resource room teacher's opinion) they ever had at that middle school. His successful development exemplifies the complexity in evaluating a learning-disabled student's ability to achieve in the regular school setting. Of course, there was strong resource room support for him, but it was coordinated with the classroom as much as possible. And there was flexibility. He was included in many of the classroom activities.

In this case, desire to succeed was a strong motivating factor along with good support from home. He also had good capability to deal with school work once his disability was addressed.

At one point, his mother indicated she made sure he had his medication while he was in school. However, she didn't give him medication when he was home in the evening to limit his exposure to it. Nevertheless, in the evening he would spend a great deal of time doing homework even though it was a slow and laborious task. She requested that he not get so much homework.

The student had an open-ended program. He was going ahead on his own. It was unclear to the teacher whether there was misunderstanding on the part of the student or he simply wanted to achieve. There were no homework assignments. He was simply asked to do what he could at home. The solution was simple. The mother and teacher agreed to limit any time spent in the evening to one hour.

In this student's case and in others, a program in which the student is introduced to slightly challenging, open-ended school work within the student's capability has been very successful. He was reading on a true third-grade level in fifth grade. He grew one year in reading ability each year for three success years. In many ways his maturity allowed him to function higher than his third-grade reading level, somewhat like a bright third grader.

In fact, he scored at the fifth-grade level in some areas of reading on a standardized test while he was in the fifth grade. Whether or not that was accurate, in this case, there was a possibility the score was indicative of some ability at that level.

The double dipping occurred in the early 1980s. It made sense, was used successfully, and was classroom teacher driven. Yet, it took years to find its way through layers of state administration to be accepted as a tool to reinforce instruction in the resource room.

In fact, in the early 1970s, with the inception of self-contained special education classes, the state wanted full curriculum plans for those classes for all subjects. The curricula plans were not written from experience. There was little to none. They were written by those who were used to "kicking" out paperwork to satisfy bureaucratic penchant for paper. We were expected to also include social studies and science into the daily instruction. That eventually disappeared but it indicates the "scope and breadth" of the early promise of special education.

In the previous case, the CST was simply following protocol when they advised against including the students in the regular classroom environment. They were correctly doing what they were required to do under the guidelines of the system regarding testing. Their testing indicated little hope for these students in the normal school environment. It has turned out, over the years, that there has been too much confidence in that kind of information. It encouraged the creation of too many self-contained special education classes.

Laws and programs created at the state level did not have enough flexibility to allow for adjustments that would allow more conducive conditions at the local level. What compounded the issue even more was the amount of time it took for pertinent information to reach the appropriate level of decision-making authority.

A system in which there is more local control of the process, could have prevented the serious issues that developed. The education establishment failed education when it gave the special education bureaucracy authority to create a system of self-contained special education classes. Wholesale "mainstreaming" of most special education students came about because of a crisis, not as a thoughtful solution to a problem.

In fact, "mainstreaming" must be addressed in terms of its effect on education in general. Should CSTs have the authority to interfere with the smooth delivery of classroom instruction? The claim that they can "train" a classroom teacher to handle particularly troublesome students with some sort of in-service training is a "fallacy."

Two aspects of placing special education students in regular classroom situations must be addressed. What school resources are available? Is the student being placed in a teacher's class because of no resource room availability? That's the school district's problem. Are the other students in that class going to have their instruction limited because of a CSTs problem?

Another aspect is that CSTs have the authority to disrupt classroom procedure without the necessary expertise or sensitivity to group instruction. The need for an education authority on an equal decision-making level with the CST is necessary to protect the integrity of the classroom. It took time for the truth to surface that the longer a student was in those self-contained special education programs, the further behind they fell in achievement.

The wholesale mainstreaming that ended most of those self-contained programs though faulty was better than continuing the classes. How many students were relegated to self-contained special education classes in which optimum development was denied is impossible to know. What is known is confidence in the extended use of self-contained classes in special education eventually came to an end.

CSTs were in complete control of those classes because of the law that created special education. The concept that created that flawed approach must be revisited. The way in which mainstreaming special education students from the resource room are assigned to the regular classroom has the potential to have much influence on instruction in that classroom.

If the special education students are mainstreamed into classroom groups where they can take an active part, they would be well-served. To place them into a classroom with an aide to "supposedly" help them be part of a group, or with an aide to supervise some independent work, would be a disservice to the class and the student.

An aide would be more helpful in a resource room where a group with as much as eleven students could be assisted. As the students work independently, the aide could circle the class as well as the resource room teacher and work with students who have completed their school work and are ready to have it discussed. Sitting in a class waiting for one student to complete school work or even helping that student before he/she has had a chance to make some independent decisions is counterproductive. The student should be doing school assignments at that student's independent reading level.

Testing by a CST results in information concerning certain aspects of learning disability. In the case previously discussed there were aspects of normality not discovered by the CSTs' testing. That is not the only weakness in the process. The indiscriminate use of aides in the regular classroom has the possibility of disturbing classroom instruction to an unacceptable level.

Using aides in the resource room has the effect of assisting students with grade-level work designed specifically for that individual. Having a classroom teacher supervising an aide assisting a student with individualized school work is something that could be done in a resource room more efficiently. A resource room student in a regular classroom for group instruction with an aide is a waste of time and money.

Individual instruction materials that a student must read and then interpret directions bypass a most common weakness in perceptual disability, the student's inability to absorb and interpret oral discussion. If the student is at a level where that is not a problem in a regular class setting he/she does not need an aide.

If a school authority such as a principal or the classroom teacher realize the efficiency of an aide's assistance in a certain situation, then an aide should be used. CSTs should not have the authority to decide whether, or not a regular classroom program will be adversely affected by their actions, that decision should be up to the school principal.

Another failure of the special education bureaucracy was the transition to a full day of instruction for the special education program. Initially, special education self-contained classes began with a four-hour day in which the teacher was with the students from the moment they arrived until the time they left. Eventually, the state mandated a full day of instruction. Tumultuous conditions were created because there was no transition period.

Lack of adequate supervision during the lunch period resulted in behavior problems that affected the program for years. Without proper supervision for the full time they were in school, special education students learned to act out in a manner which was never allowed under adequate supervision. Special education classes got used to turmoil that had never occurred in the past.

It soon became apparent to special education teachers the CSTs did not appreciate the severity of the situation. There was an aspect to running a classroom that was not part of their understanding. The only place the CST could turn was to various kinds of intervention strategies from books. A "saving grace" would have been more of an understanding of the problem on the part of the special education department. Extreme measures were needed to correct the situation. That never happened.

The recommendation, herein, that classroom teachers have more influence in decision-making would have made a difference in the everyday life of all those involved. Regular school authorities would never have allowed the tumult that followed the change in the school day for the special education program. Threat of special education law kept regular school authorities at a distance.

It would have made a difference then and it can make difference now, if the practicality of running a classroom is taken seriously. The offer of providing in-service support to classroom teachers who are chosen to include a particularly difficult student into their program is a "joke," one that is not so funny. It really is cover for a CST that doesn't realize the difference such extreme moves make in the lives of teachers and regular class students who deserve the best education a school district can offer.

There is a better way in which CSTs and resource room teachers can work together, especially in elementary schools, "more resource rooms." A first level or first stage IEP not covered by state law could be a transition between special education and the regular school program. It is conceivable that a first level of recommendations could help a special education student move successfully through elementary school without constant reevaluation and close surveillance by a CST.

Interim reports by staff involved with the student could take the place of state-mandated meetings and reports. That kind of an approach would certainly free up CSTs to concentrate on cases that are more serious and when necessary require a second stage report that would follow all the protocols of state law.

In twenty-seven years of this teacher's special education experience there was only one occasion when a psychologist sat down and essentially counseled a student. The student was in a class for the emotionally disturbed. He asked to talk to a certain psychologist.

The call went out. The psychologist arrived at the school and talked with the student. Apparently, the same thing happened on a few occasions in the past. The psychologist related that for some reason the student wanted to talk to him at times. There was never any kind of counseling setup with the student.

A program of some counseling by the psychologist of the CST would be of benefit to the school district. Any program that would relieve them from so much paperwork would probably be considered as relief. If the profession was created to be of assistance to humanity, those trained in it would welcome the opportunity. Surely there is a need in society.

When classroom teachers at the elementary level make a referral of a student to the CST, there is usually an intervention period, an LDS (learning disabilities specialist) offers some suggestions that may improve the situation. Discussions with experienced teachers indicates the LDS rarely has anything new to present. If the experienced teacher explains they have used some intervention, that should be enough information for the CST to go to a next stage.

One of the big mistakes of special education protocol was to underestimate the experienced classroom teacher's fund of strategies that help make lessons relevant. Before they make the decision that the student needs some service the school has to offer, experienced classroom teachers have already exhausted their "bag of tricks."

When an IEP is produced by the CST, state law mandates procedures that are costly and time consuming. The CST then has some authority over the school program because of its right to decide on placement of the student. Many times, especially when the student thrives in a resource room situation, there is little need to keep producing the paperwork required by the state mandate. Sometimes parents use the IEP for reasons outside the original intent of the law, and being bolstered by the law, cause a time-consuming and costly problem for a school district.

A simple solution would be to begin with an interim IEP that depended on the resource room teacher, the classroom teacher, and an authority within the school, such as the principal, to make education decisions that guide that student's progress through the school program. There are explanations in other parts of this book that discuss the resource room teacher providing a curriculum for each subject the student is taught in the resource room.

Students with varying diagnoses can easily be accommodated in resource room programs where the instruction is most often individual. The use of aides in the resource room allows a special education teacher to supervise up to eleven students. Individual assistance geared to that student's needs can be carried out in a more efficient manner. If that aide sat next to a student in class ready to help as" needed," there is a waste in time and money.

That is why there should be an education authority that can make decisions regarding the way in which special education students are included in regular classroom programs. The state structure, with laws they believe cover the matter, is too far away to also preserve the integrity of adequate classroom instruction for all students. Finland along with special education, provides for psychological and guidance counseling in elementary school, all of which is controlled at the local level.[1]

At a time when more state aid reimbursement for students identified as emotionally disturbed became available more than the usual number of students were identified as emotionally disturbed. The maximum number of students identified as emotionally disturbed allowed in a class by law is eight. However, the number of students in the class could be raised by one-third to eleven with permission from the state and the addition of an aide. We could never figure out how the state decided that one-third of eight was three but that was the law.

The class about to be discussed was made up of eleven boys. Originally, two girls were assigned. A recommendation that it would be inadvisable to have them in a class with these boys was accepted. There was no class available to which they, the girls, could be assigned so they were put into the regular school population. One of the girls eventually became the vice president of her senior class.

The class was made up of too many tough cases to get any consistent positive patterns going. This teacher had to work outside the limits of the usual school day to make sure no emergency situations arose. For example, attendance on the school grounds by the teacher was necessary when their buses arrived. It was also necessary to stay with them after school until their buses picked them up.

Going out of the building for lunch could only be done after arrangements were made for either the principal or his head teacher to watch the class. Without strong supervision this group could fall into chaos in a moment's notice.

Normally, that kind of work is challenging but rewarding. However, the program that resulted required so much control of behavior that the opportunity for instruction was limited. The administration had stacked too many students with serious behavior problems in one place. Since the state gave more state aid for students identified as emotionally disturbed at the time, there was no good reason to have so many of them in one class. It was another case of a failure of leadership.

Personal experience with special education students at that time pointed in the direction of learning problems. Students identified as emotionally disturbed had less problem functioning in school when their education was guided by an individual learning program.

There is no such thing as marking time in special education. Special education students are best served as an integral part of a regular school program That means they should be part of a school where the goal is to offer as much mainstreaming as possible.

The situation concerning the class for the emotionally disturbed previously described denotes a failure of education leadership on more than one level. The special education administration created a class that limited potential. The school principal tolerated a poor education situation because the lines of demarcation between his areas of responsibility and the areas of responsibility for the director of special education were poorly drawn.

The township was receiving the maximum amount of benefit from state aid without regard for the well-being of the students the aid was supposed to help. Finally, the state was allowing the students to be stacked in classes above the number in their own rules and regulations regardless of the effect on the learning situation.

There was never any program that included consultation with the classroom teacher before the makeup of the class roster or suggestions for the future at the end of the year. There was no good reason to extend that class roster to eleven. The original eight students in the class were very tough to deal with.

The reason the students in that class behaved in a turbulent manner was the move on the part of the state to extend the school day for these students. It resulted in chaos, not just for those students but for all special education classes. It occurred in the early 1970s when special education programs consisted mainly of self-contained classes.

The original special education program in the state was a four-hour day for the students. Continuous supervision by the classroom teacher was a necessary part of the program and not appreciated until after the state changed the rules and regulations regarding the length of the school day.

It was decided at the state level that the special education programs were to be the same as regular school programs regarding the length of the school day. So little information was given to the classroom teachers that, initially, they thought the local special education administrator had brought about the change.

There were no meetings, planning sessions, or even discussions. The extra time was added to the school day and aides were hired to supervise lunch periods. Lunch turned into a disaster for just about all special education classes. The negative results on behavior lasted for years.

Those who planned the move failed to consider that times when classroom teachers were not in charge required equally qualified personnel to be in control. It was disastrous "change" created by poor planning on the part of leadership. A report of what happened to the class can serve as a guide to the effect the change had on many other special education classes in that position.

The original class consisted of eight students. Before the extension of the school day there was a mutual respect among the students that was a result of a stable class situation. Instruction was for the most part individual and the students worked adequately on their own to complete their school work.

One boy was an interesting case. He came as a nonreader even though his age was around twelve or thirteen. He and his mother had been living out of a car before they came to live in our school district. He refused reading instruction until his mother came to the class and observed his reactions. She sat next to him and told him to listen to the teacher and cooperate. His cooperation was begrudging but he did finally accept reading instruction.

The problem with providing instruction was his advanced age. Most material for beginning readers was not appropriate for him. In addition, he was self-conscious about his inability to read. He accepted cartoons as a starting point.

The Nancy and Sluggo cartoon strip was used to provide visual meaning to accompany the words. The first time he read for meaning was a time when the daily cartoon was placed in front of him and he was asked to read it silently to himself. He read it and laughed, obviously understanding the joke involved.

The preceding description was an attempt to put a real face on the situation about to be explained. It was this student and others like him that were most affected by what happened. Before the change in the school day he was always in a controlled situation. School for him and the others in his class was as positive an experience the teacher could provide.

After the change, that was gone. The lunch period provided by the system was a wild and unruly affair because it was not supervised by anyone with the control of the classroom teacher. It was a time in which arguments and fights were a daily occurrence.

That affected how the students acted the rest of the day. The boy previously mentioned and others like him had a chance to revert to behavior that they never had a chance to show when the regular classroom teacher was in control. In addition, they were able to learn a thing or two from each other. Any positive results the program may have provided in the morning were lost. A good deal of class time each afternoon was spent trying to compensate for the negative effects of the disorganized lunch.

Self-contained special education classes were never the same. The disruptive lunch periods were a negative factor that persisted for years. A solution required not only resources but also recognition of the severity of the problem, which never happened.

Surprisingly, the special education department never appreciated the seriousness of the situation and continuously tried only limited interventions to calm things. That highlights one of the defects in the organization by the state that permits the special education department to have so much control over education classes.

The individual reports they produce on students do not deal with the total program and the classroom teacher's need to run a classroom with an adequate program. Those reports do not address the delivery of services in the classroom situation. Thus, the resulting intolerable behavior on the part of the students was considered by them to be just another thing the classroom teachers would have to deal with.

The classroom teachers were the only ones to appreciate the fact that their students were in a much more serious and debilitating position than they had been before the move. If there were local control of education and an education element that could adjust CST decisions, a better education situation would have resulted. The board of education would never have tolerated such a situation had they been the agency with appropriate authority.

Principals had only an ill-defined control over special education classes. Some principals were reluctant to become too involved, other principals stepped in when they saw a need. Yet, there was only so much a principal could do in that situation regardless of his level of concern. The problem had to be recognized and solved at a higher level. But to allow the disruptions as tolerable on the part of administration was another failure in leadership.

This failure in leadership highlights the true source of most of the problems. It's the system. Poor leadership on the part of a few people could not cause the wholesale disruptions that occur. Most of the leaders involved were competent and wanted to do well. For the most part, it's what the system demanded of them that led to widespread problems.

The education establishment has control over a system that has preempted teachers as the base in education, not considering them to be the best source of reasonable "change." There has got to be a better balance between education as a bureaucracy and education as a personal relationship between teacher and student.

Teachers should be accepted as influential members of the community in which they teach, not just employees who can be transferred at will. That concept will also be addressed later in this book. After all, there was a time when teachers were considered by state law to be in the place of parents when the children were at school. The main change in the interim is the increase in the bureaucracy that controls education.

Presently, local school programs are dominated by state regulations, the education establishment, and teacher union values. A lack of student achievement seems to have been the result. Local control of education relying on programs in which experienced classroom teachers have influence, as in Finland, would help bring back realistic focus on achievement.

More local control of education would help bring serious thought to solving problems that is not hindered by layers of administration and the time it takes for such problems to reach an appropriate decision-making authority.

A "one-size-fits-all" solution created by a state agency could be one reason why education in America does not seem to be developing the answers necessary for positive movement in education.

Education will have to be corrected from the "ground up," not from the "top down." Correction in programs will be more efficient if they are made to satisfy a local need. Lack of specificity is always a problem when attempts to control are too distant to try to cover too wide a range of possible outcomes.

State guidelines of a general nature will free education to develop more appropriate solutions to various problems as they are revealed, if local officials are given some freedom to act independently.

NOTE

1. Sahlberg, *Finnish Lessons,* p. 40.

Chapter 8

Teacher-Initiated Change That Has Stood the Test of Time

During the mid-1960s, President Johnson initiated federal legislation that encouraged classroom teacher developed programs that involved educational development for those children considered to be economically deprived. Accepted programs were given grants to carry them out. It was done on the county level and did not have to go through the local school administration. A physical education teacher from our local high school applied for and received a grant. He brought this teacher into the process in order to find a way to use the grant on the elementary school level.

The physical education teacher wanted to use students trained in his leadership program in a positive way. President Johnson's wish to enhance the education of economically deprived students offered an opportunity to do it. The teacher figured his students could best be used in the elementary school.

We came up with the idea of using them at the kindergarten and first-grade levels. There was information in the schools that indicated which students might be in the category of economically deprived. Low-income families had been identified in various ways in order that they may receive assistance. It was easy to identify students who might qualify.

The grant moved into motion at a meeting with county officials who monitored it. In order for his idea to proceed in the school district, we had to present it within the parameters of what would be acceptable in a classroom situation. The idea was to have the leadership students assist designated students with their school assignments,

The first step was to receive permission from officials in the school administration to talk to first-grade and kindergarten teachers and present the program to them. The administration was skeptical but allowed us to talk to some teachers. The teachers were surprisingly amenable to the idea. It was the era of "change" and teachers were often accused of not accepting "change." Yet, personal experience has proved otherwise.

A charge often leveled at classroom teachers in the 1960s was, "they are impediments to change." Experience with teachers presented with "change" that makes sense, is the same as what happened with these teachers. They accept it. The "old-time" principal with forty years of experience in education accepted "change" in the reading program in 1963. These first-grade and kindergarten teachers were accepting "change" in the period between 1965 and 1966.

The fact that experienced teachers can easily tell the difference between reasonable education decisions and deficient education programs is easy to understand. Teaching in a classroom has them considering many kinds of variables in different situations on a daily basis. One of the biggest challenges is deciding between competing issues, which has the most valuable "pay off" for students.

With proper respect for the value of "the teaching experience," society could have been spared many of the problems created by "top-down" management. Deciding what to emphasize as important and what is not important on a daily basis is part of administering a classroom program.

In this case, assisting designated students with their school assignments was something that would help a classroom teacher deal with a roomful of students in a more efficient way. That was obvious to these teachers. They were allowing other people in their classrooms for the first time ever and were embracing the concept because it made sense.

The program began with six aides who were able to report to the elementary classes early in the afternoon. They spent time assisting students for the last two periods of the elementary school day, working one on one with the identified students.

Immediately, the students who were receiving assistance were seen in a positive light by the other students in the class. In fact, the other students began to ask the aides if they could be helped, too. Teachers reported a rise in the status of the students being helped among the other students in the class.

Evaluation of the program was a questionnaire given to the teachers asking them to report their conclusions as to the effect of the program on the students who received the daily assistance. All the teachers believed the students included in the program gained in, what at the time, was described as self-respect. Self-image might be more in line with current thought.

Initially, there seemed to be a hands-off policy on the part of school administration. Once the teacher received the grant, care was taken by school authorities to cooperate with him. Usually, any kind of locally created "change" would have to include the whole township.

In this case, the township may have been intimidated by the fact that, for the first time, they were dealing with the federal government. They probably wanted to tread lightly until more was known about dealing on the federal level.

In general, education has almost always gone in the direction of those in power wanting everyone to be on the "same page." It's one of the ways the state controls the education process from a distance. It's the way the modern superintendent views leadership. For example, school principals are now considered as part of a "team" as opposed to being considered the education leader of their individual school.

All elementary school students having to use the same text for a subject guarantees unanimity. Some of those in leadership positions have taken regimentation to the extreme degree of insisting that a certain elementary school subject be taught in all schools at the same time.

In this case, it's a good bet that the local school administration did not appreciate the lack of complete control that resulted, with this grant. "Top-Down" management was starting to emerge at that time. It didn't take long for the administrative structure to begin to step in and try to make something else happen. An administrator from the central office tried to offer a complaint that there should have been some sort of benchmark assessment to prove success rather than a questionnaire.

Surely, he understood students are not qualified to administer standardized tests.

To expect the classroom teacher to administer such a test would defeat the purpose of the assistance. It didn't happen in this case because testing was out of the question. The aide program was such a success that it exists to this day in expanded form.

Actually, the administrator's involvement was a harbinger of things "on the horizon." The new thought of administration in education, regarding "change," centered around theorists. Therefore, "change" had to come from higher education for it to be considered worthwhile.

The whole idea from our teacher perspective was for the program to offer positive assistance to the classroom teacher. What good is a program that requires a classroom teacher to produce paperwork to satisfy the bureaucratic tendency to push paper around?

A good example of excessive paperwork is the requirements of CSTs to produce so much in written reporting. Excessive time and energy is expended in the name of keeping track of students under their jurisdiction. They are an army of highly qualified professionals who never bring their skills to the benefit of students in anything other than a testing situation.

The original charge to special education was to make a difference with students with more of a hands-on approach. What has resulted is a bureaucracy without clear demarcation lines as to where their responsibilities begin and end. That, in turn, created some doubt in education leaders in regular school programs about how to proceed in certain situations. School principals do not always have a clear idea how to proceed in matters involving the CST because responsibility regarding school law is not always clear.

In this case, regarding high school aides, the administrator seemed to be wanting the classroom teacher take over some kind of testing regimen to measure the value of the assistance. Testing by aides or anyone else never became part of the aide program. It was the "Top-Down" approach beginning to gradually lessen classroom teacher influence in education matters.

The aide program was the impetus to have the township create the position of coordinator for federal funding. Movement in that direction was inevitable. In order for the township to take advantage of the funds that were becoming available from the federal government someone had to keep track of all the paperwork necessary to satisfy federal requirements.

The aide program which exists to this day in that school district had its origin in the aide program initiated by a local high school teacher. It was "change" that stood the test of time. The administrator who took charge, in true "Top-Down" fashion, never asked for the goals and only commented on the lack of a benchmark approach.

How can classroom teachers in this day and age have an influence on education in their school district? Very little opportunity exists where classroom teachers can influence curricula in their local school district in a meaningful way. Even though they possess valuable knowledge concerning the needs of the school district in which they work, there is no official mechanism by which they can communicate that information to decision-making personnel on the board of education.

Action by the education establishment has minimized the notion that such information could be useful to a school district. They supported the narrative, "we need better teachers" by instituting the need for teachers to renew their teaching license through in-service seminars every number of years. It is a sham and discourages school boards from looking to their teaching population, especially their experienced teachers, for information on how the school district could move forward.

Presently, teachers have no professional means to communicate their opinions or objections to a decision-making body such as the local board of education. Their practical knowledge and opinions on education issues is a wasted resource. Administrative prerogatives, grievance procedures, and even curriculum committees can become adversarial and defeat the purpose of directly communicating education information that would assist in sound decision-making on the part of the board.

There is a way in which classroom teachers could furnish valuable information to their board of education in a cordial atmosphere. A simple one-page report on curricula created by the teachers of each school, maybe even at each grade level, delivered directly to the board of education would create a record that would be most valuable to the school district. That record could be a good starting point for all kinds of decisions that would affect local education. It would serve as a guide to more effective and efficient action in the future.

It would also serve as a counterbalance to one-sided information the board might receive. That counterbalance is needed because the management model that has evolved since the 1960s has increasingly put management in a pre-eminent position at the cost of the influence classroom teachers once had in their profession. Much of the information brought to school boards from outside a school district is slanted by a point of view or an ideology.

A good example is the program pushed by the education establishment that has been taken up on television, "we need better teachers." That point of view comes from areas of education that profess expertise in classroom instruction. Society is inundated by the slogan. Millions of people see it on television all the time.

An administrative argument exists that claims there are poor teachers, and in-service instruction addresses that fact. If there are too many poor teacher, that is an administrative problem. In that case, "We need better administrators," should be the slogan. School administration has that responsibility but rarely, if ever, is it addressed.

One of the most difficult classes with which this teacher had to deal was one of eleven special education students, with an aide (one-third more of a class of eight students is eleven). At the time, the state was paying an extra amount of money to support the class. They allowed the expansion of the class size to the detriment of the students.

The classroom teacher was the only one to realize these students were in a poor learning situation. One of the dynamics involved was a lack of appreciation of a reasonable classroom learning protocol by the special education bureaucracy. The classroom teacher was never consulted about the make-up of the class. That situation would never occur if there were more influence and decision-making authority regarding special education by regular school authorities. Does society need a better classroom teacher in such an instance or more local control over education decisions regarding local students?

The education establishment produces information that it believes is superior to anything that would come from local classroom teachers. Yet, in the previous instance, a conglomeration of state control, school principals as a "team" without clear lines of authority concerning special education, and CST control over classroom situations combined to create obstacles to learning for many students.

No one benefited from extension of class size from eight to eleven. Being satisfied with control over a class of students with serious behavior problems has nothing to do with effective and efficient education. It has everything to do with ignorance regarding the way in which effective and efficient education can be delivered.

Presently, boards of education have no official way to communicate with their classroom teaching staff on a scale large enough to produce a body of information that accurately reflects local values. Local control of education and all the benefits that it could bring to an individual school district must start somewhere. It can be achieved with accurate information that reflects local concerns: feedback from classroom teachers.

Information gleaned from such a relationship would be invaluable to school boards in making informed decisions regarding the successful delivery of instruction in their school systems. Such information could also serve as a basis to help create curricula that more clearly defines the school district's needs, as opposed to mandates from the state that try to fit every school district into one limited category.

The one-page curricula report previously mentioned is quite doable in the present school environment. No state mandates limit the amount of information a school board might elicit from its teaching population. The report would make school board members more of an integral part of its education community. The unfiltered information from all segments of the classroom teaching community could lead to even more specific ideas about the benefits and direction of more local control of education.

The teacher aide program was created by teachers for teachers. It was done before "we need better teachers" was offered on television. In those early days "teachers make a difference" was a popular thought. In fact, teachers will make a difference if they are given the opportunity.

Chapter 9

Poor Leadership in Real Time

The aspect of leadership that failed in the next two cases had to do with too much confidence in the promises of the special education community. The first case occurred in the early years of special education, circa 1970, during a visit to a class in another school district. The district had an especially good name for providing a wide range of special education classes.

During the visitation of a class for the emotionally disturbed in another school district, the classroom teacher was observed playing chess with one of the students. He talked about changing behavior in the students. Yet, there were no specifics.

He didn't have many students and spoke of doing a better job of changing behavior if he had fewer students. He was a teacher. He should have been teaching. He didn't have the credentials to be attempting to change behavior outside of the teaching situation.

There seemed to be no sense of purpose in the students. It looked like an approach that let students do what they wished as long as they didn't get out of hand. Hopefully, the district's reputation was not based on the fact that it was simply providing a lot of special education classes without regard to quality of instruction.

It was not known if this special education teacher had been a regular classroom teacher. There probably would have been a more defined sense of purpose if he had experience in a normal school setting. For that reason, the belief here is that he was trained in a special education program. In the early years of special education there were not enough regular classroom teachers to fill the ranks of the expansion of special education programs. This class was indicative of system failure of the teacher, the supervisor, and the administrator in charge of special education.

The transition in psychology from focusing on abnormal psychology to more of an appreciation of normality took place from the 1960s through the 1970s. Since there was little reliable foundational information, special education had a lot more promise than results in the early years.

The second case involved a class for the emotionally disturbed. It was the final assignment of this teacher's career in education. There was an aide for only eight students the sign of a problem situation in the class. The township only provided aides when the number of students in a class exceeded eight. There was an abundance of art materials, so much so that most were given to the art teacher to make room for some school supplies.

The students were very low in achievement. Two of them were of fifth-grade age reading on a first-grade level. Individual programs were created for each student. The aide worked with two students who were of fourth-grade age, working close to grade level. In addition, the whole class had a reputation for being unruly.

During the early years of resource room instruction there were a few sixth graders who were reading on a second-grade level. Within a few years, most students were almost never more than two years below their grade level in reading. That can be attributed to identifying students with disability as early as kindergarten and assisting their development with resource room assistance.

The reading levels were so low in this class that a beginning phonics program was appropriate for most of them. Even the two students working with the aide enjoyed the phonics practice. Everyone loved the group phonics instruction, especially when they took turns trying to sound out given patterns of word endings, using the various letters of the alphabet as the beginning sound. This was essentially part of the training Orton and Gillingham espoused in their program for helping students with reading disability.

The students also responded well to group sentence and story writing, both first-grade activities. The group instruction was a good example of how that specific kind of activity can be appropriate for different ages and grade levels in one class. There are not many activities that cross that boundary.

They progressed once there was organization and an individualized curriculum. Two students had a curious reaction to their own progress. A boy reading at a very low level balked at his reading program which was on tape. He was making progress and he didn't seem to want it. A girl who was functioning on a higher level started to act out when there was an attempt to get her to agree to being mainstreamed for a subject in a fifth-grade class.

They had become accustomed to a situation in which little was expected of them. They had developed an institutional behavior in which their special education class was a refuge from the world, not a base from which they could experience the outside world.

The class had been one in which there was constant trouble. Other teachers and the lunchroom aides made comments concerning that fact that the class now was showing good behavior. The biggest change regarding behavior was most likely expectations. No big adjustments to control behavior were instituted.

When it was time to go to the lunchroom, the class would have to wait until the line was straight and there was quiet before they were permitted to continue. Before long the lunchroom line was self-correcting. In class they were in appropriate individual programs and accepted the school work routine. The shame is that they were so far behind academically. Their previous routines were inadequate. They related that they didn't have to do schoolwork Friday afternoons.

Each of the two cases discussed in this chapter was a failure in leadership. The person in charge, whether it was a supervisor or principal, was not providing the necessary oversight to make sure an adequate education program was in place. The time frame between these two events is about thirty years. The first one can partially be attributed to the times. Special education was expanding and there was quite a lot going on, especially in the creation of self-contained classrooms.

The second case indicated that thirty years later there was still a lot to be accomplished regarding adequate instruction. Higher education at the college and university level must share part of the blame for inadequate special education leadership. They were too far from the mainstream of education in their philosophy.

Methods and techniques of instruction recommended by the CSTs took for granted the need to face disability with what they considered as adequate special education recommendations. Experienced classroom teachers discover areas of normality in the student and build from there. The students of the last class discussed were apparently victims of special education techniques outside the purview of normal instruction. There was obviously an attempt at art therapy.

The statement was made elsewhere in this book that early on this teacher discovered the fact that if one is to develop verbal abilities one much teach them. Perceptual training did nothing for verbal ability development. Orton indicated that the sight word approach for students without a strong differentiation between the hemispheres of the brain could have the student bring into play the nonverbal hemisphere to the student's detriment.

Surely, there is enough information in the literature indicating that one is to be very careful about the development of programs for the learning disabled. Higher special education has been too cavalier about programs that are supposed to help students under their aegis. Special education students should be kept as close to normality of instruction as possible.

State officials eventually appreciated the need for special education students to be more closely connected to the mainstream and mandated it as a last resort. The state, though almost twenty years too late, realized something had to be done.

A best guess is that pressure concerning acting-out behavior forced the issue. However, there was also a factor of poor education development in that special education system. Since students in those programs were usually not required to take standardized tests, that information was most likely delayed for a long time. The idea that, "the longer a student was in special education classes the further behind in education development he/she became," surfaced in conjunction with the wholesale mainstreaming.

Special education supervisory personnel varied in their approach to what they required from teachers under their guidance. Those with the closest connection to higher special education were still discouraging the use of pencil and paper in resource rooms. The teacher was to stand in front of the room and teach a lesson. The expectation influenced some principals in the mainstream when they evaluated resource room teachers.

There is an explanation in another section of the book that describes what happened when a principal took that approach in a resource room of eleven special education students from four different grade levels.

More local control of education offers the use of professional first-hand information of the learning programs in a school district. It offers the board another aspect of consideration when decisions must be made about the curricula.

The superintendent is a person with the skills needed to approach the State Department of Education requesting various freedoms from mandates that would allow changes in special education protocol. For example, that person could explain to the state the need for education decisions involving special education resource room procedure to be changed.

Setting up an individual education plans (IEP) not governed by state law in its first stage would allow CSTs to concentrate on second-stage cases. The large number of perceptually impaired students within one or two years of their grade level could easily be accommodated in the resource room. Their programs should be individual with interim reports to the CST.

Experience with those programs showed basal learning materials (grade-level material equal but not the same as books used in the regular classroom) to be quite adequate in two ways. First, they are more challenging than special education materials and therefore developmental.

Second, they better prepare the student for inclusion in regular classroom programs by making the student more familiar with the requirements therein. Since the resource room teacher is a trained special education teacher, special materials can be used when the situation presents itself.

A first-stage IEP would also solve a problem caused by the fact that an IEP is covered by law. Some parents argue against losing the protection of the IEP even when their child is on or close to grade level. Parents could still argue to keep the protections of the IEP. But two things would make a big difference. The parent cannot easily threaten to bring a lawsuit and an administrator would have some decision-making authority in the matter. Special education theory condoning such attempts at art therapy as previously described was taking the field in the opposite direction it should be going.

Regular classroom teachers with the right kind of support from the resource room can deal with a wide range of learning problems and behavior disorders. That is why there should be an education element on the elementary level that is on an equal footing with the CST. IEPs do not need to begin with the backing of state law.

In both cases discussed in this chapter, the difference between special education expectations and those of a classroom teacher couldn't be more obvious. The first case indicated failure regarding classroom instruction. There was none at the time of the observation. The second case indicated the theoretical basis of art therapy, if that was the intention, was a failure.

The special education bureaucracy has accepted too many different theoretical attitudes toward instruction. That happens because the IEP is grounded in law and precludes interference from regular school personnel. There is more normality in students than most IEPs indicate. It makes more sense to start a student with normal instruction and use special education techniques as needed.

Too much confidence in the special education information sponsored at the state level resulted in the school district of the first case building a complex dedicated to special education classes. As previously discussed that school district was in the forefront of developing special education classes as if that alone solved the problems of educating learning-disabled students.

The highest levels of special education, in line with the disciplines involved, looked at special education students outside their realm of normality. Instead of controlling school programs, they should have been in more of an adjunct position. A resource room teacher trained in special education with regular classroom experience should be more of a central figure in the elementary school.

The authority given to the special education bureaucracy intimidated local boards of education. Situations that developed, considered to be "hands off" to regular school authorities, would never be condoned in normal school situations. Indeed, in some situations school authorities stepped in when they perceived a need. Those actions were taken in individual situations not as an official protocol.

The resource room used as a first step in special education assistance can bring the normalcy of the regular class into the picture. It frees the CST from almost endless paperwork, and most importantly, keeps the board of education as the leading education authority.

Chapter 10

Special Education as a Bureaucracy

While teaching one summer at a state institution, opportunities arose which presented the chance to attend a few staff meetings where a team of professionals brought together their information and made determinations for the court about children identified as delinquents. The team at the institution consisted of a psychiatrist, a psychologist, a social worker, a nurse, and a teacher.

That kind of interdisciplinary approach was quite different from the CST approach used in schools. When the team at the institution made their determination, their work was done. The court placed the child and responsibility was then turned over to the people or institution in charge.

On the other hand, in the public school setting of a school district, the CST retains jurisdiction. Their report carries the weight of state law. That puts them in a quasi-supervisory role in relation to the special education teacher who is working with the students they classify. The state has miscalculated the effects that the psychologist and the learning disabilities specialist might have on students in the team approach.

Large numbers of students are classified by these teams. Yet, they do not have the time to give each student anything more than a cursory amount of attention. The team's control over the classification is not justified by the little amount of time they have for each case. If these professionals are to use their disciplines to help with the development of students, then they should meet with students in more than the testing situation.

If time constraints and heavy caseloads limits them to identifying students who have characteristics associated with learning disabilities and making a few suggestions on teaching strategies, then their jurisdiction should be limited, especially in those cases which involve the learning and language disabled once identified as perceptually impaired.

The learning disabilities specialist's report of the IEP (individual education plan) is one that offers information on learning problems and strategies for improvement. It's an outline of deficits found by the LDS through testing. The special education teacher provides a curriculum and the deficits are addressed therein. The emphasis is upon the authority of the LDS by the fact that the report that results from the testing is a legal document.

Yet, after the report is delivered to the special education teacher the LDS has very little contact with the student. The special education teacher meets with him/her daily, providing instruction within the scope of the IEP, but perceiving the student's progress in a broader outline of education.

> If an education formula could be constructed to cure learning disabilities, then "prescriptive teaching" would rule the day. At one time that was considered as a wave of the future. The head of the special education department, a psychologist, envisioned it in a discussion. The fact that it never occurred can be attributed to the fact that it was not realistic.

However, it does give one some insight into the kind of thought that went into the creation of special education. Dispelling "prescriptive teaching" was a first step in a learning curve for special education. More must be done to bring it into a better alignment with the main stream of education. Some first steps have been taken. Realizing the limitations of the effect of self-contained classes for some special education students was one of them. That occurred when the state mandated "mainstreaming."

How appropriate is the attempt to fit each student into a category then approach the education of that student within the category? It would make better sense to appreciate the reality and allow for some responsibility in decision-making to an education element in the school and the school system. The extreme legal ramifications of the IEP can be a distraction that is unnecessarily expensive and time consuming.

The instruction of many students considered learning disabled is really controlled by their need not their classification. It's really the curriculum not the IEP that helps the student progress. The student's reaction to a curriculum provides more of a basis for instruction than the recommendations in the CST report.

Most parents are grateful for the help provided to their child, that would probably not be provided without intervention. However, under the present circumstances the special education teacher and the board of education are left in a vulnerable position. Even though that teacher is in daily contact with the student and provides the major part of the service provided, anyone can use any part of the IEP to cause a problem for that teacher.

In this teacher's experience, there was a meeting with a child advocate, initiated by the parent, concerning line 18 of page 5 of a 9-page IEP report.

It mentioned a teaching technique not used by the teacher because it was not necessary. The student could perform the schoolwork in question on grade level if there was adequate study. The advocate even offered a bit of an apology by saying she was sorry she had to have such a meeting.

Nothing resulted from the meeting, except that the school system was inconvenienced that afternoon. It was a case of something that happens too often in special education. The parent wanted to keep the designation of the IEP on the student's record. In this case, there was a lesson for the township and special education. There is need for more authority connected to the board of education.

In the previous year, an older more experienced classroom teacher had recommended the student be removed from the special education protocol. Most of the student's schoolwork was adequate, either on, or close to, grade level, when he studied.

The teacher in charge during the next year was less experienced and quite intimidated. In more of a political gesture, she acquiesced to the mother's demands. The student was kept on the special education rolls and received a half a period of resource room instruction each day.

The less-experienced teacher should not have been put in that position. The CST made a political decision that was not in the best interest of the school system because they were overruling the decision of the more experienced teacher. Going with the current teacher's decision was wrong. An education authority such a school principal, under a new set of rules, could have taken the pressure off the less-experienced teacher and made the decision without threat of a lawsuit.

An IEP was used by a parent in a most extreme way because there are no safe guards for the local school board. A handful of professionals spent a few hours in consideration of something that could have been handled in a better way by the correct professional in a few minutes. This case was the least amount of problem that can be caused with an IEP and a parent with an ulterior motive.

All ramifications of the IEP were not considered when the special education bureaucracy was given so much power. That occurred when special education was at its height of influence and all the "promise" was in "full bloom." Local school boards of education should have been delegated some discretion. As boards of education assume more local control of their education programs the situation with special education will have to be addressed.

Perceiving resource rooms on the elementary level as a compromising zone would be an excellent area for special education to blend with the mainstream of education. If only the deficits reported in the LDS report are addressed by the special education teacher there would simply be a remedial situation. That is not the expectation.

When a special education teacher takes over responsibility for a student's reading, language, or math that teacher must provide a curriculum. Such a curriculum is usually a collection of relevant grade-level materials appropriate for the student which provide for a year of academic development.

Sometimes, students have more competency in areas the LDS found to be extremely deficient. A few times over the years, there have been problem situations because the student showed abilities that were supposed to be limited according to the student's instructional plan.

A first-grade student was assigned where the determination was made that his auditory processes were so weak he could not take advantage of phonics. Therefore, no phonics were to be used with the student.

During an observation by a supervisor, there was an accusation that phonics was being used because the student was heard trying to sound out a word. Letters were written to the CST about his auditory abilities, indicating he seemed to have more than the report recorded. Gradually permission was given to use phonics. Letters were more efficient than conversation because they became part of the student's file and the teacher was willing to put his judgment in the record. A bureaucracy is finely tuned to written records that are a part of an individual's file.

At the end of the year, testing by the speech teacher indicated the student's auditory abilities had developed quite a bit, which was most likely due to maturation and some phonics training.

Why would instruction in phonics be so clearly disavowed at such an early stage in a student's development? That exposes a weakness in the CST approach that categorizes the student as being in a certain area or areas of deficiency. In fact, Orton claimed learning disabled who are denied phonics training are not helped, maybe even harmed.[1] He was addressing an approach that concentrated only on learning sight words. Yet, it would be good for professionals to realize the nonverbal hemisphere of the brain could be involved when it comes to learning disability.

If there were no follow up on what was apparent each day, the student would not have received the best advantage of what the school program offered. However, once again the teacher was vulnerable, this time from the wrath of the CST and the supervisor. He did not have the freedom to automatically take the student where those abilities directed. The IEP could have become a limiting factor in that student's future.

Optimal local control of education would indicate a closer relationship between a board of education and its teachers than that which currently exists. Boards of education "hear" from all segments of the community. Yet, the part that knows the most about the children of the community, classroom teachers, has no meaningful line of communication.

The special education bureaucracy has a semiautonomous relationship with the school program. A school system must answer legally to what are "recommendations" for instruction. State rules and regulations regarding special education students could be adjusted to fit less monitoring of students functioning in a successful manner.

The state should at least revisit the circumstances around the concept. Special education in Finland covers need rather than classification and almost half the student population receive some sort of assistance before they get to what we would consider the high school level. They focus on assistance very early in the education process to allow for a student's optimum development. Each student's instruction plan can change from year to year as the need changes. That is accomplished within the structure of the school program for the year.[2]

Our special education went through a similar learning experience upon the inception of resource rooms. Before the sixth grades were assigned to middle school this teacher had occasion to work with some students in sixth grade who never had assistance. There were reading levels as low as second grade. Within a few years there were almost no students more than two years below grade level in reading. Early intervention with resource room programs worked very well, even with students in kindergarten.

There is another aspect to the use of IEPs that deserves some discussion. A few parents want their child to be covered by the IEP even when the student is working close to, or on grade level. They want the protection of the IEP to retain an aspect of control over the school system. Any student close to grade level should be responding to expectations. The IEP in such situations should not be covered by state law.

Hopefully, with the advent of more local control of education, the board of education and classroom teachers would have more "say" over such situations. A school principal with the correct decision-making authority could be a buffer between CST decisions that unnecessarily and adversely affect classroom programs.

Let the school principal decide on the best learning situation for all involved. Individual programs available in the resource room provide a good learning atmosphere for the student and allow the classroom teacher to provide a good learning situation for group instruction. Individual instruction in the resource room provides for the best and most efficient development of skills in those who are identified as learning disabled.

NOTES

1. Orton, "The Sight 'Reading Method' of Teaching Reading as a Source of Reading Disability," 135–143.
2. Sahlberg, *Finnish Lessons*, p. 47.

Chapter 11

IEP as Legal Document vs Classroom Teacher Day-to-Day Evaluations

Some classified students, namely those diagnosed as learning and language disabled (LLD) once identified as perceptually impaired, would be under a more correct jurisdiction if they were assimilated into the normal school setting, under the control of regular school authorities, after they have been identified. The avenues that best prepare them for being kept in the mainstream of education are those programs that are most similar to the regular classroom.

There is no problem teaching students to work independently using regular class materials appropriate for their reading level in the resource room. The key is having a range of materials from which to choose, along with individual instruction. The experienced resource room teacher is fully capable of making or obtaining special materials if necessary.

In providing a curriculum for the student, the special education teacher is doing more than just addressing the issues in the report of the CST. That curriculum is the next stage in the student's development. The daily interaction that occurs is the most important part of the student's education.

By compensating for the student's deficits, finding areas of competency, and providing appropriately challenging school assignments, on a daily basis, the special education teacher is in a position to affect the student's development not available to the CST. Yet, the CST report takes precedence. There is not enough weight given to the special education teacher's work with the student.

Most CSTs easily defer to the special education teacher when reevaluations take place. That is done because most CSTs realize they are dealing with the heart of the program. However, that respect for the resource room and the special education teacher's position there is on a case by case basis. The resource room is an important part of the elementary school program. Much more important than the state assumed it to be at the time the regulations and laws were brought into existence.

The resource room teacher's role in providing a curriculum is not appreciated in the rules and regulations of the state. The IEP does not and should not denote a complete special education program for the student. The special education's flirtation with self-contained special education classes that began in the 1970s was based on a mistaken concept that special education programs could better deal with learning disabilities in a confined setting. Mass mainstreaming was the result when the truth was revealed, too many years later.

There is some indication the special education teacher in the resource room is going to be brought under even more control by the special education system in the future. In the final year of this teacher's career there was a meeting at which a special education reading textbook was introduced that was to become standard the next year. All resource room teachers were to use it for reading instruction.

Almost twenty-five years after resource rooms started providing instruction for perceptually impaired students, the special education department starts to get the idea there is a curriculum involved. The use of a text is probably some kind of organizational move which most likely would have the result of institutionalizing the students in the program and relegating them to less than optimal achievement.

One might notice that the standard text would lend itself to grouping. Grouping, with repetition and reinforcement, has been shown to be advantageous to slow learners. Perceptually impaired students are a different matter. There is a good deal of what one might call "scatter" in their intellectual abilities. They may have delayed development in some academic areas. However, testing can show less ability than the student possesses by focusing on those areas of difficulty.

It is in the classroom with the teacher and an appropriate learning program that focuses on other abilities that foster intellectual development. Individual instruction increases the student's ability to deal with the written word. Group work institutes the very condition that makes classroom instruction for the learning disabled such a problem, inability to deal with various aspects of auditory processing.

Special education grouping in Finland changes each year and is connected to the school curricula.[1] In America, the resource room offers individual instruction. Individual learning plans in Finland would be connected to the grouping that occurs within the lower-elementary school structure. Our approach would more directly satisfy the individual needs of the student and should offer a better long-term advantage to each student.

There are some aspects of repetition and reinforcement that can help learning-disabled students. However, we now know much more about how to allow them to maximize their abilities than we did when special education started years ago. Individual instruction is one of the keys.

In the early days of special education, supervisors with higher degrees encouraged what might be called "fads," most likely from theory. One example was the idea of not using "pencil and paper" to teach in the resource room. The direction to stand and teach a lesson might be appropriate in a classroom where repetition and reinforcement with a group are called for, but it is not appropriate for the resource room where students from different grade levels with different programs might be in attendance.

Experience told this teacher very little was understood and retained when there was discussion with resource room students, especially with group lesson presentations. The most efficient education took place when the student first made a consideration, like reading then following directions. After the student has made some decisions based on the interpretation of directions and completed some or all of the work, the teacher and the student then had a good starting point from which to make the lesson relevant.

Since the assignments are open-ended, the student doesn't have to wait for the teacher's correction to continue. As problems arise they are addressed in short order. Unlike the learning materials in the regular classroom that continue on to the next lesson, learning materials in the resource room offer basal programs that present a variety of practice on the same concept.

In twenty-seven years of special education teaching only two instances stand out where a program of daily discussion seemed to fit a certain group of students. Standing in front of a room and teaching a lesson to one person at a time where a group of five students might be present, each in an individual program, is not very productive.

One of those times has already been discussed. It was the use of phonics instruction to the especially low functioning class for emotionally disturbed students. That kind of activity did take place at other times with other students but did not constitute a daily routine.

Another occasion was with a group of resource room students in an elementary school. They were all poor readers and did not visualize what they read. They were like students referred to earlier in this book in that they had difficulty making illustrations of what they had read.

There was an attempt to have these students practice some sort of visualization by having them close their eyes and try to make pictures in their mind of what the teacher was describing. They related to the theme, "going to the river" very well. Each day, with heads on desks and eyes closed, the students would tell about an adventure on "the river," many times including others from the class in their story.

There was another instance where five students in fifth grade seemed to be on about the same reading level. An attempt was made to teach them in a group using the school's fourth-grade text. One boy could not be scheduled at the regular time, so his program was individual. The group was not very productive but the boy in the individual program seemed to develop more self-confidence and responsibility.

The group seemed to get bogged down with the introduction of vocabulary and group discussion. They would have been better served with individual programs, focused on each student's learning problem. Group activities were special attempts to achieve a goal that seemed to fit each individual situation. The last one discussed was not as successful as the others.

Students from the resource room who showed continuous improvement did so because of the complete individual program presented by the resource room teacher. The IEP was a starting point, not an education program.

An appropriate education program is made up of learning materials gathered by the resource room teacher that allow for the intellectual development of the student. Basal learning materials (books, worksheets, and so on on the same reading level of the student in the individual program except that they are of the same type of learning materials used in regular class instruction) are plentiful. It is easy to find materials that a student could handle independently once that student can read above the second-grade level.

The experienced teacher can offer a much better developmental classroom program than that offered by the special education materials. The special education practice teacher referred to previously, claimed her college program did not include the use of individual instruction in the special education classroom. That was the early 1970s. She was surprised by the use of individualized materials, so her story was most likely true.

Certainly, the lack, on the part of CSTs of understanding the severity of the change in behavior that accompanied the introduction of the full school day for special education students was a sign that their individualized expertise took for granted classroom procedures.

The skill of successfully using classroom procedures in teaching is something that contributes to the development of a classroom teacher. Lack of understanding on the part of the CST is displayed when students are placed in a classroom with an aide with the expectation of the classroom teacher to "oversee" the situation. Along with the offer to provide in-service for that teacher.

This classroom teacher began using individualized reading and math instruction before 1965. One of the earliest reading materials conducive to individualized reading instruction was published by *Reader's Digest* in the 1960s. Those materials were used at the state institution of previous reference.

The education supervisor at the state institution was impressed and decided to order them. He appreciated the fact that, three or four books on each grade level from third grade to eighth grade allowed for immediate instruction simply by having a student read in books until a comfortable level is apparent.

The following experience was the result of what a new principal expected to see according to some special education guidelines. Apparently that principal was impressed by the special education directions that the resource room teacher should stand and teach a lesson to the class in lieu of students using pencil and paper to supplement instruction. The following occurred during a classroom visitation, for purposes of teacher evaluation, by that school principal.

There were eleven resource room students in the room. Because there was an aide present, one-third of eight the usual number was, allowed to be, added to the class roster. There must be an explanation somewhere that explains the state's consideration that eleven results from one-third of eight.

At the time, there was some talk that special education teachers were to stand in front of the class and teach. It had something to do with the "no pencil and paper" idea. The principal expected to see the resource room teacher stand in front of the room and give a lesson.

The aide sat at computer with a first-grade student who was a nonreader. The other students sat at desks doing individualized work. The teacher spoke to students one at a time correcting completed work with appropriate comments. In the evaluation that followed the visitation, the principal criticized the teacher for not teaching a lesson in front of the class.

The teacher's comprehensive response in the form of a rebuttal resulted in immediate reaction by the assistant superintendent. The fact that there were students from more than three different grade levels was not in accordance with state law. Within a week there was another resource room teacher assigned to the school for a half-day.

Common sense would demand one to at least develop conversation about what went on during the visitation. There had to be some question in the mind of the principal as to the "workings" of the resource room. The principal's response was much more in line as the member of "Top-Down" management.

Goldhammer, a researcher of note in education regarding classroom supervision, believed teacher evaluation should contain a conference with the teacher before an evaluation observation. He believed a discussion concerning what the teacher would like to achieve during the teaching lesson would be valuable. A later conference would involve a discussion rather than a checklist that seems to be popular in these times.[2]

He came from a generation of education researchers who believed there was variability in the way in which instruction could be successfully carried out. The segment of the education establishment that now believes their way is the best way to teach is doing education a disservice.

A recent report indicated evaluation of the type proffered by Goldhammer now occurs. The question of expectation of the evaluator comes to mind.

Is there an appreciation of the individuality of the teacher or are there expectations of what is presented in the recertification seminars?

The reason for an immediate response on the part of the resource room teacher in the case previously discussed is the same as the response in written letters to the CST concerning phonics instruction. Administrators realize the written record is a powerful tool. If there were no opportunity to document the situation, there most likely would have been no action taken regarding the conditions in that class.

Resource room instruction functions within the school's curricula and is closely connected to what happens in the classroom. The CST and the IEP deal with individualized information. The resource room is more naturally and closely connected to the school program than the classification process of special education.

It would be more reasonable to consider resource room instruction closer to the regular school setting by having a first stage IEP not governed by state law govern the situation. If a student has problems beyond resource room placement, then a second CST report could result, with a more intense look at the student.

Within the regular school setting, the school principal, with precise agreement as to the extent of his/her authority, could be a mitigating factor that more clearly defines the demarcation between the regular school setting and the responsibility for the individual student on the part of the CST. Such an arrangement would more easily fit into local control of education.

The school principal in dealing with the IEP of an individual student not covered by state law would be on equal footing with the CST. The resource room student would be in a more natural jurisdiction since the resource room teacher provides the curricula which not only addresses the recommendations of the IEP but also provides for the student's overall development.

Without the need for continuous CST written reports in a successful continuation of the resource room student's movement through the elementary school, more resources for direct instruction to students would be available which could be used in a variety of ways.

A word on frontal lobe development of the brain might be appropriate at this time. Within the past few years information has come forward that indicated frontal lobe development may continue into the mid-twenties for some people. That was significant news for those of us who are interested in the effect of frontal lobe development on the learning process of individuals.

One of the things learned from the original personal research on handedness discussed in other parts of this book was the frontal lobes of the brain begin to develop between the ages of twelve to fourteen. The significance of frontal lobe development, according to some researchers, is that they offer some higher-level thinking to the person. In the case of the perceptually impaired, (now LLD) that development could offer alternative pathways to learn things that were difficult when they were younger.

Concerning the most current medical and scientific information, there will be much to consider regarding maturity in the future. This teacher, with the original information on frontal lobe development in mind, asked parents of perceptually impaired students if they had learning problems when they were in school.

Many times, at least one parent would indicate he/she did. The next question was, "When did things start to get better in school?" A majority indicated during their sophomore year in high school "things started to come together, and school became easier."

Since almost to a person, the parents indicated sophomore year in high school as the point in their lives when school became easier, it's not much of a stretch to consider frontal lobe development is involved. In fact, such a development could be the reason why some people can learn to read as adults when they couldn't as children. "Late bloomers" in many instances are probably benefiting from frontal lobe development.

There is a great deal of discussion ahead. The effect on what is considered maturity seems to be changing before our eyes. What is the significance for schooling? It's a strong argument for keeping the student as positive as possible regarding school and as close to the mainstream as possible. Special education students in middle school felt stigmatized. That's probably one reason they had a tendency to act out. Consider that same kind of reaction in high school students.

Students might have an easier time "fitting in" as learning becomes easier in high school. There is now a number of new things to consider about the various stages of a young person's life. It opens up new avenues to guidance counselors.

There is a limited place for grouping in the resource room. It could be accomplished with some beginning phonics, group language instruction, and some other specialized activities. However, individual instruction is the backbone of the program. Yet, the CST never got into the particulars of how instruction was delivered. There was never much discussion about the theory or reasons for the manner in which services were delivered.

This experienced teacher's approach was to develop programs in which the student was encouraged to become as independent as possible with his/her schoolwork, do as much as they could before the teacher got involved. It was specifically designed to deal with students with varying abilities and from various grade levels in one room at the same time.

There never seemed to be a complete understanding or interest on the part of the CST concerning the day to day activity in the classroom. Their individual approach to learning didn't seem to incorporate classroom management as an important consideration. They seemed to believe it to be a natural by-product, instead of an important part of the teaching situation.

Hopefully, with local control of education, there will be more flexibility in state law concerning decision-making at the local level. It is not necessary to back all CST and IEP reports with state law.

The resource room in the elementary school can be a place where state control is minimized, paperwork is eliminated, and a relationship between the school district's responsibility for the student and special education's responsibility is more clearly defined. A good start would be to make the resource room student more of a regular class responsibility with the principal as a decision-maker in place of the CST.

NOTES

1. Sahlberg, *Finnish Lessons*, p. 47.
2. R. Goldhammer, *Clinical Supervision* (New York: Holt and Winston, 1969). *IEP as Legal Document vs Classroom Teacher Evaluations*

Chapter 12

The Teacher as Facilitator vs Goals and Objectives

Early on, in special education, the head of the department related that he envisioned the day when testing would reveal the exact deficits of students and they could be plugged into the exact programs that would correct those deficits. That was "prescriptive teaching." It was supposed to be "change" in special education. That was the assessment of a psychologist, the head of the special education department at the time. His focus was on diagnosis. He was saying the teacher didn't matter as much as the CST testing. He believed the teacher was there to merely carry out a program designated by the CST.

Prescriptive teaching was another "new idea" that was eventually discarded. But it does highlight some of the thought that went into the creation of the CST approach. There was an expectation that the application of their disciplines to the education process would go beyond simply testing and classifying students.

Experience pointed this teacher in the opposite direction of what the special education administrator believed. Each day with a special education student is an illumination. Constant adjustment of his/her program is beneficial and necessary. A good deal of planning time each day was spent adjusting programs and seeking out appropriate materials.

The administrative personnel, of the special education department, did not seem to understand the disconnect between their diagnosis of deficits in relation to the special education resource room teacher's need to provide a curriculum. The belief here is they had stereotyped assumptions and never really developed an accurate understanding of the day by day work in the resource room.

In fact, the most debilitating action to our program ever taken was the insistence from a special education supervisor that we write goals and objectives for everything we taught. It will be explained in more detail later but there couldn't be a better example to show how little understanding there was on the part of the special education department of the needs of the resource room.

Personal attitude toward resource room instruction with the perceptually impaired centered on some observations made during early contact with them. Their responses to group instruction and discussion was guesswork, always attempting to pick up some clue as to how to respond. There was not much consistency in their day-to-day responses to what was previously taught. It became apparent there was too much day-to-day confusion to create some continuity of understanding.

For the teacher to have confidence instruction is efficient, the student has to show more involvement and understanding in the process at the initial stage. Therefore, after students had second-grade reading skills, there was more emphasis on independence. Learning materials were provided that contained the need to study a skill then read directions as to the use of that skill in an exercise.

They were introduced to the routine of an independent program. If they could handle it completely on their own, they did. If not, they would receive only enough guidance to get them started in making some of their own decisions. Once the student was comfortable with the routine he/she would proceed at his/her own pace. Corrections and discussions were the teacher's main work once the student had completed his/her task. If need be, there would be added practice. However, if the student showed good understanding, he/she was encouraged to move through the program at a good pace.

On the other hand, one concept that came from those who were influenced by higher special education was, "Special education teachers should not use pencil and paper with special education students." They should be using other alternatives. The "other alternatives" varied. At times, it included things like poor attempts at art therapy. In the early days of special education classes, some people had the students doing things that had more to do with arts and crafts than skills development.

One of the first things learned upon entering special education was, "If you want to develop verbal skills, you have to teach verbal skills." The perceptual training, we did with young students, did nothing for their verbal skills. Being criticized for using pen and paper and work sheets in the resource room did nothing to further the efficiency of our programs. That's why there is the conclusion of poor leadership.

As resource room teachers we, at times, had to survive from one fad to another, depending on who was in charge. It might even "boil down to" where the supervisor's concept of the special education student and the needs of such students was "born." Those of us who came from the regular classroom had a tendency to concentrate on normalcy. How much of a normal school program can the student perform before special education techniques are introduced to the student?

Special education personnel with advanced degrees in special education tended to gravitate toward special education techniques earlier in the process.

When a CST first contacts a teacher seeking some intervention for a student in their class, a usual first step is to explain some strategies to the teacher that might help the situation. It's not uncommon for the teacher to explain that has already been tried. Classroom teachers know what services can be provided. When they ask for intervention, they are asking for the service not for a discussion. It's been reported that now the CST will accept a list of alternatives tried by the teacher to expedite the process of classification.

A reference has already been made to the difference between classroom teachers in special education and their leadership involving attitudes toward alternative teaching procedures. Special education teachers with experience in the regular classroom want to see how much in the way of regular class procedures and materials could be used with a student before going to alternatives.

There are many areas of normality in a student diagnosed as perceptually impaired. Special education administrative personnel had too much confidence in alternative teaching methods. The teacher must provide for the student the best program which the student is capable of handling. If that means activities more along the lines of mainstream education, then that would be to the long-term benefit of the student.

Using the student's initial independent response to instructional materials sidestepped any confusion occurring when students had to deal with auditory directions. It gave him/her the responsibility of deciding what to do. He was required to create a mindset to the materials thereby allowing for a realistic starting point of discussion or consideration.

It developed more understanding and confidence in the student in dealing with written directions. It also developed independence because the student could continue working in the program with a minimum amount of direction from the teacher. In fact, the concept is along the lines of the teacher as a facilitator.

Carl Rogers a psychotherapist of note perceived that to be the natural role of the teacher. His value to education lies in the fact that he emphasized learning as central to individual development. Personal involvement and meaning were two things he deemed necessary for learning to take place. To him, lecturing and direct instruction were too rigid. He reported a great deal of initiative and industry among some students when they were free to pick their own direction and do the work they wished. He attributed that success to the freedom of choice.

The freedom of choice he perceived is not conducive to the public school setting. However, a good deal of initiative and industry is produced when students are given open-ended work and encouraged to move along on their own. They did not need the freedom of choice that was envisioned by Carl Rogers as the prime motivator.

His concept of the teacher as a facilitator fits very well with the role of the resource room teacher. He envisioned a real person to person relationship, a basic trust in the learner, and a sensitive awareness to the learner.[1]

A good example of working along those lines involved a boy from Russia. His parents came to America when he was very young. He entered school without command of the new language and had some problem with mathematics. We came together in a resource room class while he was in the seventh grade. By that time his behavior and self-confidence had been affected.

He had a defeatist attitude toward math and a tendency to follow group behavior. A regular fifth-grade math textbook was used. He could handle the work independently and found math was not as difficult as he perceived. After his computation improved he started to move along quite well. He was asked if he had ever finished a book. The answer was, "No, are you kidding," meaning, "I could never do that." As he improved the idea of finishing the whole math book arose in him. He started to work more and more at home.

One day there was a call from his mother. She was very nice and asked if this teacher could talk to him about the math. She knew he was not getting math assignments but apparently, he was not doing his other homework. He was only doing math at home. She wanted to see if he could be persuaded to be less compulsive about the math book.

It was not that easy to get him to back off. He was conquering something he thought he could never do. And he was determined to go all the way and finish the whole book. He would only agree to skipping the extra practice for each chapter at the end of the book. With pride and self-confidence, he eventually finished the book.

It would have been interesting and helpful if information of his early school history were available. Rules about access to the findings of the CST changed over the years. The whole report was only available to the resource room teacher if there was a special request. The student may have been in a different school system in a "new math" program with emphasis on terminology, which would have been doubly hard because of the language differential.

That highlights another area in which education has changed. Access to achievement test scores also became a bit of a problem over the years. It was limited and did not allow for a resource room teacher in my position to evaluate the programs used with a student the previous year.

Since there are reports that teachers are still required to write goals and objectives in their lesson plans, it might be appropriate to visit the subject at this time. They came along during the time when there was talk about accountability in education that became connected to behavioral objectives in the business world. The highest levels of the state commission of education defended it as the application of good psychology and good education theory.

Educational psychology always seems to skip the fact that "sound psychological and educational thinking" must show positive results in the classroom before widespread dissemination. Madeline Hunter, a psychologist, had a program that offered the type of control over the classroom that resulted from the use of behavioral objectives. She offers seven basic elements, "that must be considered in the design of effective lessons."[2]

She claimed to have translated the most relevant information from psychology, education, sociology, and neurology into ideas for education. That information, according to her, is the articulated knowledge upon which sound education decisions can be made.[3]

The program is an administrator's dream. It offers training for teachers on how to incorporate the seven basic elements into lesson planning. It's called the teacher decision-making model. Teachers are trained to use the basic elements by trainers who then monitor the classroom and offer feedback on the effectiveness of the use of the basic elements.

She belittles beginning teaching as learning by trial and error and offers her conclusions as, "articulated knowledge that wasn't available in past years."[4] Yet, experienced teachers couldn't get the program going after trying for four years.

Our state mandate for classroom teachers to use goals and objectives in their planning seems to have come from an interest in Hunter's approach to teacher improvement. Their confidence is by no means universally accepted in the education community.

A college professor commenting on behavioral objectives calls them a "charade." The professor claims he has run various in-service workshops for over 2000 teachers. A show of hands has indicated teachers consider behavioral objectives a burden done to keep some administrators happy.

He believes contemporary research indicates that effective learning requires a highly individualized and flexible mode of instruction. Behavioral objectives make it difficult for teachers to be flexible enough to meet the needs of individual students. They represent an attempt to provide some accountability in education and are steeped in the beliefs of educational psychology.[5]

The program created by Madeline Hunter, a psychologist, is so wide spread it is probably in every state. An evaluation of a four-year study of the program in California indicated a decline in student achievement scores in the fourth year. According to the authors of the study, "The most plausible explanation for the fourth-year decline has to do with the coaching of teachers, an area that received a great deal of attention, but perhaps not enough."

The teachers who received coaching as to how to implement the elements of the approach did not receive, in their estimation, enough coaching to make their use of the guidelines automatic.[6] Sounds like the old excuse, "not implemented properly," or in this case not supported enough. The accountability that was to be achieved didn't materialize, as the schools involved in the project moved on to another project after four years.

Her program was criticized in another article because: 1. Hunter has not produced the research evidence to support her claim for improved learning; 2. on John Dewey, a finding that might be scientific in psychology is not scientific in education until it has been tested in education practice; 3. without improved learning there is no scientific basis for the Hunter model.[7]

The final report of the Napa County Project for grades two to four significantly favored the control groups over her experimental classes in reading. There was no difference in math.[8]

A disconnect between resource room instruction and the application of the goals and objectives rule couldn't be clearer than what happened in the next situation. A teacher in the regular classroom teaches five or six subjects in a day, probably writing one goal for instruction to a class of twenty students. Writing a goal and objective for each class should take only a few minutes. Writing goals and objectives for everything we taught in the resource room was time consuming.

We were directed to write a goal and objective for everything taught to each student. And it had nothing to do with our programs. With individual instruction the student initiated the assignment. The teacher reacted to the student's work. A goal and objective for each lesson was secondary to the student's reaction to the lesson and really was not appropriate to the instructional situation. Therefore, there was no sense spending valuable school time writing one goal and objective for each lesson.

It was too time consuming with no pay off. If there were eight students a period for five periods a day, at least forty goals and objectives had to be written for the day. That was, at least, two hundred goals and objectives for the week. And in many cases a student was taught more than one lesson in a teaching period.

It literally took hours to complete these plans. They had to be done in school because you needed all the materials the students were using to do the work. And the plans were useless. They existed only to satisfy the administrator.

The shame of it was we could no longer spend the time with students that we once did. Before the change, planning periods were spent adjusting programs and when necessary bringing together more appropriate materials for students. Extra time would also be given to students whenever possible.

After the change, all that was gone. The emphasis was now on getting the goals and objectives written. It was an unbelievable waste of time and resource. Multiply that waste by the school districts in which special education teachers were forced to do the same thing. It's inconceivable that many districts initiated that policy. Yet, there is no way to know how many did it.

This was another case of the vagueness of some areas of responsibility regarding school principals and special education. A new special education supervisor was able to step into the situation and demand the plans be written. Why? Because of the distance between the place where the decisions are made, the state department, and the place where they are to be carried out, the local school district.

Administratively, they are miles apart. It would be very difficult to explain to the state commission office that students are denied service because of their mandate. Who knows how long it would take or how many levels of administration one must negotiate to even get to that point. With local control of education, one could reach a decision-making authority in one day. People making a decision would also have the added incentive, "these are our children who are missing out."

It would not be a bad idea if a school system were an education community in which all the professionals including school board members did some teaching. Public relation skills and administrative skills would not trump classroom experience so decisively. The chasm that now exists between those who teach in the classroom and those who consider themselves as managers of the system would not exist.

Local control of education could help create such a community. If the school board of education had more control over its destiny to create more of the conditions needed to run a school system, local pride would take the place of worrying how to satisfy state mandates.

The superintendent of school's position could be a conduit with the state offices of education, working out and explaining local proposals. Discovering and using the talent within the teaching force would take the place of blindly accepting education establishment proposals that satisfy a constituency of theorists that consider the classroom mundane.

Proposals even more possible and appropriate from the teaching staff, than that which is recommended here, could round out local programs that would satisfy the immediate needs and values of the community.

It is inconceivable that something of the nature of what happened with goals and objectives could happen in a school system where there was more local control of processes. Administrators and supervisors would be more closely connected to teachers and the classroom. Trust and cooperation would be a natural byproduct of a system that was constructed from within.

NOTES

1. Carl R. Rogers, *Freedom to Learn* (Charles E. Merrill Publishing Company: Columbus, OH, 1969) pp. 3–5, 106–112.

2. Madeline Hunter, *Enhancing Teaching* (Macmillan College Publishing Company: New York, N.Y. 1994) p. 3.

3. Hunter, *Enhancing Teaching*, p. viii.

4. Hunter, *Enhancing Teaching,* p. viii.

5. David N. Campbell, "Behavioral Objectives—The Grand Charade," National Education Association (NEA), Today's Education. March–April 1976, pp. 43, 44.

6. Pam Robbins and Par Wolf, "Reflections on a Hunter-Based Staff, Development Project," Education Leadership, Alexandria, VA: Association for Supervision and Curriculum Development, Vol. 44, Feb. 1987, pp. 56–61.

7. Richard A. Gibboney, "A Critique of Madeline Hunter's Teaching Model from Dewey's Perspective," Education Leadership, Alexandria, VA: Association for Supervision and Curriculum Development, Vol. 44, Feb. 1987, pp. 46–50.

8. Richard A. Gibboney, "The Vagaries of Turtle Research: Gibboney Replies," Education Leadership, Alexandria, VA: Association for Supervision and Curriculum Development. Vol. 44, Feb. 1987, pp. 54.

Chapter 13

Local Control of Education
A Beginning

There is no question that school administration from the state level down to the local level is necessary and a very important part of this complex world. However, the 1960s promised a better future for education with "new math," special education, and middle school for young adolescents. What developed was quite different. Somewhere in this grand scheme of things, classroom teachers got lost.

The following is a personal experience that might shed some light on the disconnect between the classroom teacher and the highest end of school administration, the commissioner's office.

Some time was spent in a doctoral program at a university in order to continue investigation of a study on handedness that was done to satisfy the requirement for a master's degree. The doctoral program was entered with the idea of extending the study to students identified as perceptually impaired. It was eventually discontinued because schools stopped making students available for such studies. However, the handedness information of the fifth graders still exists as the possible basis for other comparisons of handedness.

Time spent in the doctoral program was quite an enlightening experience. The study was accepted as the basis for a dissertation. It was vetted for a second time by the psychology department of the university as a requirement to consider it as a basis for further study.

That was done because the faculty advisor wanted to make sure future information would be based on a "sound footing." A committee of three professors was chosen for the dissertation committee. One of the members was a professor of psychology because of the nature of the study.

In order for this student to immediately continue work on the study, one of the first classes chosen, had to do with research. The other students in that class were finishing their doctoral program. The class existed for the purpose of choosing an acceptable topic for a dissertation. It is usually one of the last classes taken in the program.

The study on handedness was the only one that involved statistical analysis. The other topics involved research of a different kind and were in various stages of development. Some of the students were just beginning the pursuit of an acceptable topic, others were in the final stages of their research.

Many of the students were from the state department of education. There was a "knowing" attitude among these professionals. Their behavior was properly friendly but somewhat formal. It looked like their way up the ladder was with a doctoral degree.

Their world looked to be apart from, rather than an integral part of, the classroom experience. It didn't seem like they had spent time in the classroom. They represented a layer of administration that no longer identified with the classroom.

They reminded one of people described by an uncle who had advanced into a position with a national union. He had worked for many years in a factory before becoming president of the local union that represented workers from that factory and other factories in the area.

His ability to negotiate contracts gained the trust of local union members and moved him to higher positions in the union. Eventually he was part of their national structure and had an office in a large city. He became a favorite of workers in many of the factories because they could easily recognize he was one of them. They trusted him.

He was bothered by the fact that the younger generation of union representatives didn't seem to identify with the factory workers. They preferred to "run in the circles" of the higher-ups in the companies with which they negotiated. He had a term for them. He called them "labor statesmen."

The doctoral students from the state department of education were obviously very bright. They were also extremely politically "aware" as can be demonstrated by one of our experiences.

It involved a game called "Star Power" presented by a professor who had a high degree of confidence that such games had a place in the development of students at that level of education.

The game started with each student having a certain amount of chips in their hand that indicated money. Different colors designated different values. Participants were to trade chips with other students until they were able to increase the chip value to a higher previously designated value. Every few minutes trading took place, at which time students were allowed to try to trade "up" the value of their chips.

As each trading period stopped, the teacher would announce that everyone who was successful in trading up to the correct value could join the "success" group. The students from the state department were the first to become part of the "success": group. They had immediately discovered no one was checking the amount declared to be in one's hand. This student remained in the group that couldn't figure out how to get into the success group.

These students were well prepared to survive at a level of state bureaucracy that required not only intelligence but also a high degree of "awareness." They deserve respect for their achievement and station in life. However, the system of education that has developed over the years leaves them further and further from the base they are to serve, the classrooms of the state education system.

Systems do not easily recognize the need to make changes and adjustments to the times. Better ways of moving forward develop, and if strong enough, replace them and move things in a new direction. Two actions discussed in this book sponsored by the department of education of our state indicate too much bureaucracy has developed between the state department of education and the level of education necessary to deliver a thorough and efficient education to the children of the state.

One these actions is the mandate of having teachers write goals and objectives for all lessons they teach on a daily basis. It originated in controversy. Professionals in the field of curricula and supervision called it a "charade."[1] It has been discussed in some detail earlier in this book. It has been unevenly applied in the field. Common sense allowed some administrators to ignore it, when possible.

Basically, it was an attempt on the part of the office of the commissioner of education to develop some accountability and direction for teachers to improve service in the classroom. The Madeline Hunter approach was widely accepted around the country because it was highly organized and had an excellent pedigree concerning the most modern thought in psychology, education, and science. Using goals and objectives in the planning for instruction came from the thought that the Hunter approach brought to the state commissioner's office.

Its use in special education denied this teacher and others a more efficient way to deliver their programs. It was another case in which some administrators were intimidated by the fact that special education had such a close connection to the state department of education and authority was not delegated in as clear a manner as it should have been.

Another action had to do with state and local administrations working together to create and implement a transfer policy that, in the words of one central office administrator, "emphasized the fact that teachers work for the township."

The actual target was schools where teachers had a great deal of influence because of their long-term relationship with students, parents, and parent-teacher organizations. Teachers with the most influence and the most insight into the needs of the community were targeted.

The transfer policy involved the most senior member of the staff of each school, not the teacher with the most seniority, but the teacher who had been in that particular school the longest amount of time. That person was to be transferred each year to another school.

Personal knowledge of two large school districts indicated there was only one principal who refused. He had been a principal for nearly thirty years. His concern was there would be too much disruption in the school program. He considered his senior teachers to be very important for the stability of his school staff and the school's program.

The transfer policy lasted only one year, maybe two in our school district. Without inside information there is no way to know, exactly how long it lasted. The "hue" and "cry" made it impossible to continue the transfers. The move was carried out because of the strong, "part of a team" aspect of the modern administrator. In many cases the "rock" of their staff was being taken away for no apparent reason. Their "Top-Down" commitment made them carry out the transfer.

Teachers who were most familiar with the student population and would have the best interest of students in mind were considered a problem to some forces in education. These teachers would be the best candidates to offer ideas such as those in this book that could direct a school system to appropriate local control.

The decision to transfer them had to come from a layer of state control that was far removed from the everyday life of teachers in the classroom and the smooth running of a school. Maybe the term "educator statesman" can describe an administrator who is too far removed from the everyday happenings in education.

School principals who respect classroom teachers as professionals and allow them the leeway needed to run their programs know how to balance administrative power. Personnel hired for administrative positions need to be able to identify with the teachers with whom they work. A healthy amount of time teaching is probably a good starting place.

They also need to have an adequate frame of reference to make good decisions regarding education matters. A stronger allegiance to the program of an individual school should replace the education establishment's call to be a member of a "team."

A public relations dream, very friendly and outgoing was hired to take over an elementary school in another school district. He had limited experience in teaching elementary school. Without a good frame of reference to be the leader of the school, his power was used indiscriminately.

He somehow got the idea that spelling books and language books were not necessary. He believed the teachers should teach those skills using other parts of the curriculum as a base. Such an approach is a specialized activity and may serve as a change of pace from time to time. It is not an adequate program for an elementary school. It was a large school and there were multiple classes for each grade level.

After the first year, a class that was not comprised of the best students at that grade level, received spelling grades on the yearly standardized test of skills that were better than those of a class that was comprised of brighter students. The principal found out that the teacher of that class had used the spelling book. His response was to make sure all the spelling books were removed from the classrooms. There is no better way to summarize what has happened in education since the 1960s.

Inadequate programs were established by those in power who believe they know better than classroom teachers about what is best for the classroom. "What would happen if the public learned the spelling grades were depressed?" Would the establishment call for in-service training for teachers? That has been the way the establishment has blamed teachers for what has happened in education.

A school is not a training ground for a promising administrator. When someone is in a position of education leadership without a reasonable education background too many bad things can happen. The previous case is another example of classroom teachers in a vulnerable position. In spite of the fact that the teachers preferred to have their spelling and language books, such use was denied for no good reason. And they had no recourse. Would the true story ever come out, or would the teachers be blamed by administrators "looking for cover?"

Classroom teacher influence on education processes at the present time is inconsistent. It depends totally upon how much the administration wants to allow teachers to be involved, how much "voice" it chooses to give them. One school district had a curriculum committee which had a connection to the teacher's contract and the teacher's union had to give permission to anyone from their organization who might want to join the committee. How much union politics and ideology came into play is not known. There does seem to be a conflict of interest in such a setup.

Another school district, with an excellent reputation years ago, had at that time a central office administrator who took teacher participation in the curriculum planning process seriously. There was a teacher representative from each school on the committee. At the beginning of each year, when the committee met, he would tell the members of the committee, "When those doors close we are all on equal terms."

Apparently, there were many adjustments to the various curricula as a result of the committee's actions. That commitment halted when the administrator retired. Presently, the school system, for a variety of reasons, no longer has the status it once enjoyed. The lack of teacher involvement in curricula planning is most likely one of them.

The reason teachers no longer have the elevated position they once had in education is the emergence of a" ruling class," the "Top-Down" managers. After thirty-six years in education, this teacher had a lot more skill than at the beginning of his career, yet, toward the end of it, enjoyed a lot less status in the education community. What happened during the interim period? For one, those in power wanted to call more and more of the "shots" and tried to relegate teachers to the role of "automatons."

It is not by chance that as the state has gained more and more control of the education system, dissatisfaction with that system has surfaced. Teachers as employees of the board of education, has been a theme that has replaced the idea of teachers as care-takers of children. It was such an attitude that made possible the transfer policy involving senior teachers in the various schools, a reality.

Whereas, teachers were once elevated to the position of being in place of the parent, now education authorities seem to have the attitude they know better when it comes to dealing with children in school. Why is it that some school systems are able to work "hand in hand" with their classroom teachers to create new programs and improve other programs? Is it because their teachers have been properly in-serviced? The answer is no.

The real problem in education is that all teachers are not given such opportunity. Unless classroom teacher influence in education processes is mandated it will only occur as it does now, in "enlightened" school systems where administrators go beyond the usual "lip service" of classroom teacher participation and really use classroom teacher expertise as the valuable tool it is.

Local control of education can begin with a closer relationship between boards of education and their classroom teachers. A good starting point would be a one-page report on curricula from each school in a district given directly to the board of education. The "down-to-earth" needs of the classroom would be contrasted with "visions for the future," the mantra of the education establishment, usually surfacing through local administration.

The one-page report will lead to the kind of communication needed to build a base for local control. It would better identify local needs and values. It could also lead to a better balance between political positions and education concerns on school boards.

Board members will be in a better position to articulate the needs of their school system once they have a good idea of what their classroom teachers convey, first-hand information. The one-page report is a beginning and a good base from which to build a connection to the state department of education.

Local control could actually begin with the ability to adjust something like the relationship of the resource room to the regular school program. The idea of a first stage IEP for students identified as perceptually impaired as previously discussed could improve the local structure in the delivery of education service in the ways previously discussed.

The reduction of time consuming CST reports, due to less of a need to monitor students, frees special education to do work that would benefit the elementary program a number of ways. The psychologist could spend some time counseling. The Learning Disabilities Specialist could spend time working with learning-disabled students who have more serious problems. The social worker position could become one through which guidance services could also be provided.

An alternative that would add a great deal of direct instruction to students is to exchange one CST for three or four more resource room teachers. In each instance, service to students could be increased with no addition to the school budget. It's a good consideration for the reallocation of resources, to a state commissioner's office that should be ready to move in the direction of more local control of education. It is a modern movement in education that makes a great deal of sense.

NOTE

1. David M. Campbell, "Behavioral Objectives—The Grand Charade," National Education Association, *Today's Education,* March–April 1976.

Chapter 14

Individual Instruction

A second-grade student was assigned to the resource room because he was a behavior problem in class. Every time the teacher turned her back to write on the blackboard there was turmoil and he was in the middle of it. Upon entering the resource room and walking in front of the blackboard he noticed a girl copying from it. He ducked in order not to be in her way, not exactly the behavior of an "uncaring" individual.

He was comfortable with the second-grade reading material and worked successfully with it, even doing some homework. Upon observing the student in his regular second-grade classroom, it was obvious he overreacted to a couple of other boys in the class. In fact, it didn't seem to matter if someone like the teacher was watching, he went right back at them.

There was some discussion with the student in the resource room of an expectation of better behavior. Those discussions focused on behavior in the schoolyard. The classroom behavior seemed to have a self-righteous component. He was retaliating to perceived aggravation from the other boys. Telling him to ignore what the other boys did was probably worthless at the early point in the resource room teacher-student relationship.

A lack of understanding on the part of the teacher who was at "her wits end" in the matter was natural. She tried him in the front of the room to keep him under close supervision. That apparently led to even more trouble and distraction. His desk was in the back of the room in a corner by a window, when this teacher spent a period observing his behavior. On cue, when the teacher turned her back one of the other boys harassed him and he responded in kind as the teacher turned around, only seeing his response.

A general statement about trying to be good was probably the best that could be considered regarding the classroom. He was always good and respectful in the resource room, so discussion was "low key" and matter of fact, almost "man to man." The classroom teacher found it hard to believe he was so responsive in the resource room.

Apparently, he did so little work in the classroom that the CST found it necessary to comment that they wouldn't know he could read on the second-grade level if it weren't for the work he did in the resource room. This resource room teacher was transferred to another school at the end of that year. At the Thanksgiving holiday time an appropriate holiday picture arrived at the new school from the student with a note attached that stated, "I'm being good at lunch time."

It's obvious the student was a candidate for individual instruction in the resource room. In fact, without that intervention there might have been another type of classification.

The fact that there seemed to be long-term carryover of a positive attitude for behavior in school could be attributed to self-confidence built from working successfully with his reading program. He felt that he was meeting expectations. It's not uncommon for a student to feel a sense of accomplishment when the teacher can point to the fruits of that student's labor and say, "You accomplished that." Some success somewhere in school that year helped him go forward in a positive manner. Individual instruction was most likely the key in this case.

The previous experience occurred within a resource room experience. The next one happened in a self-contained class for students identified as emotionally disturbed. A fourth-grade student was transferred to a class for the emotionally disturbed during the school year. He had been a problem in school since kindergarten. There was no explanation why it took until fourth grade to place the student. He was easily distracted and quick to react to stimuli.

The class had eleven students with an aide. It had previously been one of eight students. The students were at that time subject to the lunch periods without qualified supervision. As a group of eleven they were especially tough because they had experienced so much turmoil in the past. The head teacher and the principal supervised the class when the special education teacher left the building at lunch time.

The student from the fourth-grade class was in a tough but controlled situation. He was given an individual program appropriate for his ability level and accomplished his assignments. There were many precautions taken to limit interaction among all the students in the class, one was to tape an area around each student's desk. That more clearly showed to everyone each student's territory. Part of keeping everything under control was anticipating any kind of friction that could develop.

After about four months, there was a parent-teacher's conference as part of a yearly routine. The boy's mother was shown a stack of papers about six to eight inches high of the school work he had accomplished. She responded that it was more work than he had accomplished in the previous four years of school.

Individual instruction with a minimum amount of distraction even in a tough environment allowed for some education development. There is a good amount of positive therapeutic progress for a student in the simple act of pointing out to that student the amount of schoolwork he/she has produced. Above and beyond talking about positive behavior, a stack of school work that the student knows was the product of their efforts is a strong builder of self-confidence.

There is a good deal of positive development in students that the teacher can achieve by simply doing what teachers do best, "teach." There was something profoundly wrong with the teacher's action, in the special education class for the emotionally disturbed, who was playing chess, to which there was a reference earlier in the book. With only a few students he claimed he could do a better job if he had fewer students. Where did the teacher get the idea that it was O.K. not to carry on an education program in that situation.

Individual instruction in school systems covers a wide area and offers the solution to various problems in education. It can allow for the education of those whose behavior destroys efficient classroom instruction for a classroom full of students.

Most students can be helped by such a program, but those who have some confusion with auditory discussion or directions are especially helped to move forward in a better way. When they must bring their attention to the decision-making process by first reading and then following directions, the proper focus can occur. That leads to a better understanding and therefore a better retention of what is being learned.

In the individual learning situation, a wide range of learning materials can be explored to find which ones are the most effective with different students who have various kinds of learning problems. In the early elementary grades, it offers a much better outcome for the perceptually impaired student. At higher grade levels, such as the middle school, it offers a means to control behavior, yet, continue with an adequate education plan.

Students whose behavior destroys the effectiveness of the classroom situation can be removed for whatever time is necessary for the student to agree to change behavior and become a contributing member of the class.

Such a program would need to have a school administration take an active role in providing the conditions necessary for learning to take place. It's the responsibility of a school administration to create and maintain positive conditions for learning. Placing a student in a class, any class from lower elementary to middle school and above, that has the capability of destroying the learning atmosphere is wrong. When a CST places such a student with the promise of an aide, and especially in-service help for the classroom teacher involved it also is a "sham".

That is the exact sort of situation which demonstrates the lack of understanding of classroom procedure on the part of the CST. Their disciplines do not allow for the development of the necessary expertise involved to understand the dynamics of various classroom situations. That is exactly where local control is necessary. There must be an authority that can deal with special education on an equal basis.

The job of a school administrator "begins and ends" in such situations. Their job is to represent all students, appropriate instruction for the learning disabled, and the best possible learning situation for each classroom.

Local control of education can create an atmosphere where administrative personnel such as an administrator in charge of discipline takes control of a class designated for individual instruction. Any special education teacher familiar with resource room protocol could take part. Specific knowledge of the progress of students in individual programs along with personal contact creates a relationship of caring that is a necessary part of disciplinary action.

Expectations need follow-up. It doesn't take much commentary on the part of the teacher to say, "How are you doing?" for that student to eventually report back on his/her own, "I'm getting along better now." If they think you care they will respond positively, even if they must do it when "no one is looking."

If local control is going to create more of an education community everyone involved in the education process is going to have an active part. Teaching will be more productive if administrators can guarantee a good atmosphere for learning and take an active part as much as possible. No one sitting behind a desk can change behavior. The students of the school districts who received the most attention from all the school personnel, will receive the most benefit.

Pursuing local control will lead to freedom in creating programs that fit the needs of the local education community in a variety of areas. This book has concentrated on those areas familiar to the writer. Personal experience is one of the great teachers for those who pay attention. A cliché, but so true, is the fact that those who do not learn from the mistakes of the past are doomed to repeat them.

This book was written with the belief that systems and layers of administrative bureaucracy caused much of the dysfunction in education process that are now so evident. Knowledge of what happened can help to make sure it doesn't happen again.

Classroom teachers of a community are those who know and care for the students of the community. They can be relied on as the base from which more local control of education can be built. The breath of their experience can provide the direction for appropriate local control that would enhance the education of all present and future students. Individual instruction as presented in this book is only one of the many ways in which some local control can bring about more efficiency to the delivery of instruction to students.

Epilogue
The Classroom Teacher

The students of the 1960s would gather around teachers on the schoolyard at the beginning of the school day. By the late 1990s they didn't even look up as a teacher approached. Before the 1960s, the pedagogy reflected the best practices of classroom teachers. In the 1990s leadership was giving classroom teachers in-service instruction ostensibly to show them how to be successful in the classroom.

Social changes, with more emphasis on the individual can partially explain the change in attitude toward adults on the part of students. There was also a subtle change at the highest level of education that was not lost on parents. Teachers were once considered to be central figures in the education process, consider sayings like, "Teachers make a difference."

By the 1990s teachers were made to be the "fall guys" for the failed programs of "change" that leadership implemented. In addition, the change in status of the classroom teacher has been an evolution in which existing layers of administration sought to expand the limits of their authority and responsibility. In each case, classroom teacher influence on school programs was lessened.

Experienced classroom teachers possess more skill than most people realize, or at present, education leadership is willing to admit. With all the talk of departments within high schools, middle school multidisciplinary instruction, team teaching, and so on, there is a tendency to forget that each teacher possesses individual skills that allow him/her to run a classroom and relate to the students within. As we think of a school system being responsible for the education of our children, there is a tendency to forget all teaching has a component of individualism.

The instructor or teacher is one who delivers service in a unique way. As a teacher becomes experienced, a set of skills develops that differentiates that person from all others. The skills develop as the teacher applies his/her knowledge of pedagogy to the classroom situation. How unique and valuable is that set of skills to the education process? That set of skills, defines education. The education process as we know it depends on the people who possess those skills and could not exist without them.

The paradox of education, in the present, is that the skills and value of the individual teacher are downplayed in favor of administrative prerogatives such as a superintendent's "vision" for a school district. The superintendent's vision might dynamically indicate a desirable future for the school district that motivates the right people. However, the future, a theoretical concept, is something quite different from reality, the lessons received by students every day.

The principal of the elementary school of the first class this teacher taught was asked for advice. He had been in education for forty years. He refused to leave the classroom, teaching half a day and carrying on his administrative responsibilities the other half. He came out of a culture of education that looked to the classroom teacher as the center of the education process.

In the past teachers were chosen to be school principals after considerable experience in the classroom. Those principals were eager to take over a classroom for a day or two whenever they had the chance. His advice was, "They gave you a certificate that says you're a teacher. Go in there and teach." It was confidence in the individual. It was the realization that the educator is someone who develops in the classroom situation.

Pedagogy is not an end but rather the beginning. Education is the successful application of the pedagogy by the individual. And it is the individual's unique and personal use of the curriculum that defines education. Nothing can take the place of the classroom experience in terms of finding the best ways of developing the knowledge and skills in students that are offered in the curricula.

Leadership failed education for two generations of students when they tried to impose "change from above" with little to no input from classroom teachers. And their insistence that continuing in-service is necessary for classroom teachers to keep up or even learn new skills is more of the same.

The only memorable in-service this teacher ever attended was one in which someone who had taught first grade presented all the teaching aids she had created. It was truly impressive. However, at the time it had no meaning for seventh grade special education.

In-service instruction needs to be focused on a problem for it to become meaningful and efficient. To claim that they are going to improve teaching across the board with their program of in-service is to hearken back to the promise of many programs of "change." Both promises are outside the purview of credibility.

Supervision of classroom teachers is also quite different today than in the past. The school principal who had been in education for forty years was in and out of everyone's classroom, three, four, or even five times a day. At times, he would sit and listen. Other times, he would look at students' work and talk to them about what they were doing.

He had a comfort with, and an interest in, the basic elements of education that does not exist in the modern administrator. He could identify uniqueness in various teachers who taught in his school. Most likely the same uniqueness that researchers of the past who, in trying to identify good teaching skills, concluded there was such a variety that it was difficult to come up with one set of principles which defined good teaching.

In "New evaluation methods proposed," an article in the *NJEA Review* of November 1986, Michael Timpane, the head of Columbia University Teachers College commented on teaching. "Teaching is a complex activity. There is no one template one can use to measure a school district or teacher and say, 'This is or is not good teaching'." The occasion was a panel on evaluation that indicated, "instructional supervisory process must accommodate different teaching styles and learning situations within the context of each classroom." That was part of the "thinking" inside the education establishment in the 1980s.

Within a dozen years, the education establishment was mandating teacher in-service for teachers to keep their teaching licenses. Their increased authority over that time is another reason why education continued to move away from the classroom teacher as the central figure in education.

Pressure from the perceived failure of education policy resulted in them highlighting classroom teachers as the main reason for the decline. The power they hold over education allowed them to create their own self-serving solution, in-service for teachers.

Hopefully, there has been enough information offered in this book that indicates the education establishment and levels of bureaucracy have had a lot more to do with the lack of efficiency in education than classroom teachers, who offer a lot more to the education process than simply being, "automatons carrying out the results of the theoretical thinking of the time."

Systems and bureaucracy cannot be expected to put themselves out of business or change their direction without some outside impetus. More freedom can come, if boards of education insist on claiming some of their rights as a part of the education system that has a lot more knowledge and personal concern about local needs than the state.

A good and even natural starting point would be a petition to extend local control over some aspects of resource room instruction. An excellent argument can be made to have it exist as a program that meets special education at a half-way point. The special education resource room teacher works with the CST to provide service with a first-stage IEP not covered by state law. The immediate school administrator or school principal is in charge, and as a result, the special education student is even closer to a regular school program.

This first move can serve as a precursor to more movement on the part of a local board of education to create more efficiency in their school system.

About the Author

Vincent B. Troiano is a lifelong resident of New Jersey, born in Perth Amboy in 1937. He received a bachelor of arts degree in music from Rutgers College and a master's degree in teaching the socially and emotionally maladjusted from Newark State Teacher's College, now known as Kean College. He attended the doctoral program of education at Rutgers University department of Education and recieved supervisor and principal certificates.

Mr. Troiano taught for the Old Bridge Township School System for thirty-six years: grades 4–6 for nine years and special education for twenty-seven years. His special education teaching career began in self-contained classes working with students identified as emotionally disturbed. Concentrating on learning disabilities was an outgrowth of that experience.

www.ingramcontent.com/pod-product-compliance
Lightning Source LLC
Chambersburg PA
CBHW030145240426
43672CB00005B/272